The
Committed
Marriage

Biblical Perspectives on Current Issues

HOWARD CLARK KEE, General Editor

The Committed Marriage

ELIZABETH ACHTEMEIER

THE WESTMINSTER PRESS
PHILADELPHIA

Scripture quotations from the Revised Standard
Version of the Bible are copyright, 1946 and 1952,
by the Division of Christian Education of the
National Council of Churches, and are used by
permission.

BOOK DESIGN BY DOROTHY E. JONES

PUBLISHED BY THE WESTMINSTER PRESS ®
PHILADELPHIA, PENNSYLVANIA

PRINTED IN THE UNITED STATES OF AMERICA

Library of Congress Cataloging in Publication Data

Achtemeier, Elizabeth Rice, 1926–
   The committed marriage.

   (Biblical perspectives on current issues)
   Bibliography: p.
   Includes index.
   1. Marriage. I. Title. II. Series.
BV835.A25   234′.165   76-7611
ISBN 0-664-24754-7

Contents

To Our Children
Paul Mark and Marie Louise
for the time when they marry

Foreword

This volume launches a series of books, *Biblical Perspectives on Current Issues.* The aim of this series is to examine major problems confronting the church today in the light of Biblical revelation regarding God and his purpose and man and his responsibility. Writers have been chosen on the basis of their competence as scholars, their skill as communicators, and their deep concern for the church.

We believe that all these goals are well served in Dr. Elizabeth Achtemeier's book on marriage and the family. Gifted Bible scholar, esteemed teacher and writer, and devoted wife and mother, she brings a range of knowledge, a wealth of experience, and a depth of sensitivity to an area where conflict and confusion threaten the very fabric of society.

This first volume in the projected series deals with its subject in a most challenging and readable way. Expressing herself with warmth and candor, she takes positions that are sometimes against the stream, occasionally challenging and at other times affirming traditional assumptions. But consistently she sheds new light on perennial questions, a light that comes not only from perceptive analysis of the contemporary plight of marriage and family life, but from her thorough knowledge of the Bible and her own evangelical commitments as well.

Although this series is addressed to church professionals, pastors, teachers, and students, this volume is so clearly written that interested laymen will have no diffi-

culty with it. It is a work that has implications not only
for marriage and the family but also for such related
concerns as women's liberation, discipline of children,
and divorce. The insights it provides will clarify issues
and sources of conflict; its compassion provides healing
and renewal.

HOWARD CLARK KEE
Editor

Bryn Mawr, Pennsylvania

Preface

This book has been written for the purpose of giving a protestant testimony. It is first of all a protest—a protest against the distortions, misuses, and scorn that our current society daily heaps upon the marital relationship. Secondly, it is a testimony—a testimony of one who knows there is joy and great goodness to be found in Christian marriage, for those who will commit themselves to it. I hope that as other Christians are introduced to this book through discussion groups, preaching, church classes, and personal reading, they will be prompted to add their own witness. For far too long, Christians have remained silent about what they know to be true in marriage. The time has come to break the silence and to let a society, starving for it, hear our good news.

E. A.

Richmond, Virginia

CHAPTER 1

The Merciful Word

It is not good that the man should be alone; I will make him a helper corresponding to him.[1]—Gen. 2:18

God has spoken many merciful words to humankind. There was that explanation to the shepherd Moses: "I have seen the affliction of my people who are in Egypt, and have heard their cry because of their taskmasters; I know their sufferings, and I have come down to deliver them . . ." (Ex. 3:7–8). There is the sobbing refusal to give up even a faithless people to judgment:

> How can I give you up, O Ephraim!
> How can I hand you over, O Israel!
> . . . .
> My heart recoils within me,
> my compassion grows warm and tender.
> (Hos. 11:8.)

There is the invitation to all who hunger and thirst for more than this life offers: "Ho, every one who thirsts, come to the waters; and he who has no money, come, buy and eat!" (Isa. 55:1). There is offer of rest for our burdened selves: "Come to me, all who labor and are heavy laden, and I will give you rest" (Matt. 11:28). And summing up it all, there is that word from a dying Son on a cross: "Father, forgive them; for they know not what they do" (Luke 23:34).

Yet, in a Biblical history that overflows at every point with a divine mercy beyond all imagining, no word spoken by God is more merciful than one that God speaks to himself at the start of the story, as he muses over his creative work: "It is not good that the man should be alone; I will make him a helper corresponding to him" (Gen. 2:18).[2] God decides that we should not be by ourselves on his earth, that we should be set into a relationship. As it is put in Ps. 68:6, "God gives the desolate a home to dwell in." Into the structure of his creation, God speaks the reality that we were not meant to be alone!

In an age in which we have become turned in upon ourselves and salvation has come to be understood in terms of the development of an independent "personhood," that is a merciful word indeed. It speaks to the deepest hungers of our hearts and lifts us out of our deadly serious preoccupations with ourselves. God intends that we live in relationship with another!

Moreover, that "other" with whom he wills that we live is to be one "corresponding" to us, one who matches us, hunger for hunger, one who answers what we are, one who loves back in response to our love, who cares in return for our care, one with whom we can talk and share, in mutuality. The women's movement—following earlier church teaching—has laid an awful distortion upon us when it has rejected this verse from Genesis as meaning that woman is a subordinate servant to man and destined to be slave to his needs. Just the opposite is the meaning! Man and woman are intended by their Creator to live in a relationship of "corresponding," answering one another, body to body, mind to mind, spirit to spirit. And that correspondence is the merciful means God gives us to defeat our loneliness. "It is not good that the man should be alone."

We know lots about loneliness these days. Our age

loneliness
Contemp. living

could almost be called the Age of Isolation, for every structure of our society seems diabolically designed to cut us off from our fellows. We carry on our daily commerce in large urban centers, where we are just another hurrying figure in the crowd, additions to the traffic problem, where a smile on the street may invite mugging or rape, with no help forthcoming from passersby. We move from neighborhood to neighborhood, following the job market and pursuing success. Either we are too rushed or we move again too soon ever to know the family next door. Our children disappear on the school buses in the morning, our spouses on the commuter trains, and whole days of thoughts, emotions, and experiences go by which never get told or shared. We arrive home too tired. We have meetings to attend, television or homework takes the evening; family members remain private individuals apart, strangers in a common domicile. Those who grow old in the family circle are sent off to a retirement community, or occupy beds of neglect and pain in local nursing homes. Over it all, we paint an image of prosperity, sophistication, and importance, while underneath we know that if the rush stopped and we were not distracted —by alcohol or volunteer work or even by television football—we would find ourselves encapsuled in loneliness, beset behind and before by no one.

We hunger to share with another—to get rid of images and roles and job expectations and to be valued for ourselves. We want to converse with someone who will listen to our hurts and who will rejoice in our triumphs, to pour out the finest carings in us and to find them received and treasured, to give of ourselves in concern and labor and to have it needed and wanted. It is the nature of human life, symbolized for us in God's word in the Genesis story, that we were not made to be alone. And when the loneliness of our time becomes too much for one of us encapsulated souls, the human mind takes refuge in the escape of mental illness, or behavior becomes aberrant.

The difficulty, however, is that many have become cynical about God's remedy for our loneliness. Marriage, according to the transcendent witness in Genesis, is intended to meet our needs for companionship and relationship at the deepest level. But many are loudly testifying these days that it does no such thing. "It's not all it's cracked up to be," remarked Bill Loud, that typical California husband whose marriage we watched fall apart on the television special, *An American Family*. Apparently he spoke for thousands of Californians, whose divorce rate now equals, and in some counties surpasses, their marriage rate. Indeed, if we listen to a former *Newsweek* columnist, the interaction between modern husband and wife is itself an exercise in loneliness:

> "Both are guilty. Both are vulnerable. Both are victims. But they don't know *where* they are hurting the other, because they're never asking: who *is* the other one? Really they're speaking to someone who doesn't exist. Somebody whom they have made up."
>
> Dear Abby, have you ever heard a better description of modern marriage? [3]

For many persons, the American marriage simply does not work. In the eyes of many women liberationists it is a subtle form of slavery. To the children who are victims of our booming divorce rate, it is often a hypocritical pretense at permanence and acceptability. For many young persons of marriageable age, it is an outdated social oddity, whose pitfalls and agonizing dislocations can be avoided by the choice of an alternate life-style.

To maintain, therefore, that the institution of marriage is God's merciful answer to our need for relationship is for many people to perpetuate a sick joke that long ago ceased to be funny. Marriage in America has produced too many wounds, too many agonies, too many shattered personalities, ever to be considered by many a merciful balm for anything. In answer to the word, "It is not good that the man should be alone," thousands would reply, "I think I'm better off without the other."

Thus, like most of the affirmations of the Biblical faith, this one from Genesis confronts us amid the realities and agonies of our daily life and appears offensive, unreal, and untrue. Of course, that is the way the Biblical word usually appears to us. It tells us that "the meek shall inherit the earth," when we assume that the meek get trampled in our world of power plays. It maintains, "He who saves his life shall lose it," when we presuppose that the only way to get ahead in the game is to watch out for number one. The Biblical word always seems unreal in this world of realities. God's word about marriage as answer to loneliness seems to share in that quality of fantasy.

It is not an isolated word, however, and Genesis is not the only witness to God's desire to set us into relationship. Few other passages in the Bible can match in imagery the Genesis picture of God, the Father of the bride, bringing the woman whom he has created to the man, and the man crying out in joyful ecstasy. But writer after writer in the Biblical story revels in the marital relationship. Proverbs, the book that intends to teach the wisdom of how to get along in this world, is sure that "he who finds a wife finds a good thing, and obtains favor from the LORD" (Prov. 18:22), and so the young man is admonished, "Rejoice in the wife of your youth" (Prov. 5:18). "House and wealth are inherited from fathers," it is written, "but a prudent wife is from the LORD (Prov. 19:14), and a good wife, when she is found, "is far more precious than jewels" (Prov. 31:10). Life may be full of useless knowledge and of toil that accomplishes nothing, but even then, says the Preacher in Ecclesiastes, a man can enjoy life with the wife whom he loves (Eccl.

9:9)—apparently his marriage gives him gladness even when all else seems "vanity."

These happy reflections on the goodness of marriage might be considered nothing more than relics of a distant and more simple age, were it not that the marital relation is understood in the Biblical witness, as more than a human construction. Marriage is not viewed there as a passing social custom, invented and therefore abandonable by human beings, but a structure of human life built into creation by deliberate intention of the Creator. Jesus' words in The Gospel According to Mark point to this understanding:

> . . . from the beginning of creation, "God made them male and female." "For this reason a man shall leave his father and mother and be joined to his wife, and the two shall become one." So they are no longer two but one. What therefore God has joined together, let not man put asunder. (Mark 10:6–9; cf. Matt. 19:4–6.)

The world is created in such a way that marriage is a necessary part of it, a fact to which the universal incidence of some sort of family unit has always anthropologically attested. That there are many different types of marital relationships within the family of humankind is a further anthropological fact that is not to be debated. But the Bible testifies to this basic truth that the marital relation is a structure of creation.

The unique aspect of the Biblical witness to marriage, however, is that matrimony is presented as a joyful and good relation. The world as created by God was intended to be "very good" (Gen. 1:31), and according to Biblical faith, marriage shares in that basic nature of "goodness."

In fact, so good is marriage, in the Biblical view, that it can serve as a symbol of the relationship of the God of all mercy and good with his beloved people. In the Old Testament, Israel is frequently spoken of as God's wife (Isa. 50:1; 54:4–6; Jer. 3:20) or bride (Isa. 62:5; Jer. 2:2;

Hos. 2:16–20), and the Lord is the Husband who has entered into marriage covenant with his people (Jer. 3:20; Ezek., ch. 16; Hos., ch. 2; Isa. 62:4). In the New Testament, Jesus is compared to the figure of the bridegroom (Mark 2:19–20 and pars.; John 3:29; cf. Matt. 25:1–13), and Paul states that through faith, the church is presented as a pure bride to Christ (II Cor. 11:2). In the letter to the Ephesians, the union of husband and wife is the concrete symbol of Christ's union with his church (Eph. 5:31–32). In Revelation, when the coming Kingdom of God is portrayed, it is pictured as a marriage (Rev. 19:6–9; 21:2, 9–11).

Although we have been confronted by this testimony to the goodness of the marital relation, the monstrous fact is that we have distorted marriage to such a degree that we now find it offensive. God's merciful words are spoken to us, and we are told that the world in which we live is structured by its Creator in such a way that we are given the possibility of a relationship with a mate which can be so good that it can symbolize the quality of God's own love for humankind. Yet, somehow we have so corrupted the marital relation that the widespread reaction of our society to that gracious word is to call it nonsense and to reject its mercy!

Perhaps in cynically, or even sorrowfully, rejecting that word we act out our age-old propensity to take the Word of God by force and nail him to a cross. We seem never able to accept God's goodness to us or to receive his gifts. We end up always corrupting them, always scoffing at them, always crucifying the incarnate word. In the widespread cynicism with which our distorted society views God's gift of marriage, we crucify the infinite grace of God upon the Golgotha of our scorn.

It is as if some dreadful disruption had descended upon our landscape, twisting our purposes, and distorting our understandings. We call good evil and evil good, and put darkness for light and sweet for bitter (Isa. 5:20), in a monstrous mockery of mercy. It reminds one of that deathly silent, almost apocalyptic picture drawn by the prophet Jeremiah, in which no voice of bride or bridegroom, no sound of feasting merriment, disturbs the still of a society sick to death with the sin of rejecting God (Jer. 16:1–13; 7:29–34; 25:10 f.; cf. Ezek. 24:15–27; Rev. 18:23). Could it be that our modern rejection of marriage is the sign, as in the prophetic writings, that we live under curse and judgment, and that ours is a sickness, symptomized in our divorce courts, far more malignant than we had imagined? There is something wrong, something terribly wrong, with life as we live it. And that infection oozes out and poisons the fellowship at our family tables.

So perhaps we need to take a new look at the marital relationship and how we have corrupted it. Perhaps it is not an antiquated institution, which has outlived its goodness and usefulness, as so many in our society would have us believe. Perhaps those who advocate that we abandon marriage are the ones who are speaking nonsense, and it is the Biblical word of God after all which is "the way, and the truth, and the life." A lot of us have staked our lives and happiness on that, and we do not think we will be disappointed.

One thing is certain. God still holds out the gracious invitation to us to take advantage of his mercy. He intended for us to live in a "very good" creation, and we corrupted that goodness. Yet, even now he extends to us the possibility of wholeness and joy. Our marital unions can be made good again, our dreadful disruptions can be cured. There is no limit to the inexhaustible working of God's desire for our abundant life.

In the following chapters, therefore, we will explore the nature of Christian marriage and how it may be lived. Perhaps in the course of such exploration, some may be rid of that bitterness left in their mouths by the widespread corruption and condemnation of marriage in our society. Perhaps, too, some may discover ways that Jeremiah's promise for the future can become, in their lives, a joyful reality in the present:

> . . . there shall be heard again the voice of mirth and the voice of gladness, the voice of the bridegroom and the voice of the bride, the voices of those who sing, as they bring thank offerings to the house of the LORD:

> > "Give thanks to the LORD of hosts,
> >   for the LORD is good,
> >   for his steadfast love endures for ever!"
> >   (Jer. 33:10–11.)

CHAPTER 2

To Marry
or Not to Marry

I appeal to you therefore, brethren, by the mercies of God, to present your bodies as a living sacrifice, holy and acceptable to God, which is your spiritual worship. Do not be conformed to this world but be transformed by the renewal of your mind, that you may prove what is the will of God, what is good and acceptable and perfect.—Rom. 12:1–2

Our son is a college student, and during his vacations at home he tells us a lot about his classmates. They are apparently a fine group—intelligent, creative, hardworking—but surprisingly some of them are afraid to get married. A few of them come from families broken by divorce, and they are determined not to expose themselves to the unhappiness their parents have known. Most of them are the offspring of traditional, middle-class homes, in which husbands and wives play the usual roles of breadwinner and housekeeper respectively. The young persons' see those roles as traps of convention, in which they have no desire to be caught. Rather than run the risk of failure or of imprisoning conventionality, these young students have decided not to marry at all. Most of them will later change their minds of course, but the startling fact is that right now they are afraid of marriage.

On the other hand, there are large numbers of young persons in this country who face the prospect of marriage with no qualms whatsoever. They have just the opposite reaction: they view the matrimonial state as the magic solution to all their problems. By getting married, they think, they will solve their personality conflicts with one another, or they will get away from home, or they will fulfill their physical and emotional needs. Most of all, by getting married, they will do what is expected of them, and automatically reach that approved status of "mature" and "on their own."

The truth is that both groups are subjected to slavery. The first is enslaved by fear, the second by unrealistic stereotypes of marriage, and slaves rarely are in a good position to make rational and responsible choices. They have far too many memories of pain, far too many hungers, far too many needs to be filled to choose their course of action wisely. Yet, it is precisely within such a situation of bondage that many of our society's young people are making their marital choices. It is therefore no wonder that many of their marriages will subsequently fail.

The Christian faith is certainly no magical insurance policy that will guarantee that a young person chooses wisely when he or she is deciding to marry or not to marry, or when he or she is picking out a mate. There are thousands of marriages titled "Christian" which have also ended in divorce. But there is in Biblical, Christian faith a unique insight into the human personality and situation which can give us a freedom in our choosing, and which can bring to our understanding of marriage an entirely new perspective.

The Biblical faith affirms that we human beings can truly and fully understand ourselves only in relation to

God. There are many different ways in which our society has tried to define the human personality: biologically and anthropologically, sociologically and psychologically, economically and historically. Even the popular fads of transactional analysis and of astrology have their definitions of what and how we are, as do all the mystical movements with their various gurus. But it is the conviction of the Biblical faith that when we have talked about a person as an animal, or as an id-ego-superego, or as a product of cultural configuration and history, or as a bundle of drives and needs, or even as a rational or mystical being, we have not fully defined him or her. Human beings are first of all creatures of a sovereign Creator, who are made to live in ongoing and loving relationship with the God who has made them. Any definition of human life that leaves out that divine-human relationship is automatically going to be incomplete or distorted. In fact, affirms the Biblical faith, the health and outcome of human life are basically determined by that relationship, and the preservation of the wholeness of the living relation with God is thus determinative of all other facets of human living. Applied to marriage, then, the affirmation is that the relation with God of the marital partners—or lack of it—will have a basic influence on their union, second in importance to no other factor. In short, faith in God is not something added on to an otherwise healthy or unhealthy marriage. It affects, often decisively, every facet of the union.

The Biblical faith affirms something else about us human beings. It says that each of us is a unique creation of God, created by him for a purpose in life which each of us uniquely fulfills. That is, Christian faith affirms that human history is not meaningless. Rather, it moves toward a goal and completion which God has set for it, and each of us is created by God to take a significant and unique part in that movement, until God's will for life is accomplished and his purpose is completed.

If we ask what God's purpose is for human history, we could sum it up in the words of the Lord's Prayer: "Thy kingdom come on earth, even as it is in heaven." God desires that there be a goodly community on this earth that lives in justice and righteousness and peace under his lordship, and each of us has a part in God's work toward that goal. The nature of the Kingdom, according to all the Bible, is life abundant for every creature, born out of an enduring fellowship with God himself. In the words of Revelation:

> Behold, the dwelling of God is with men. He will dwell with them, and they shall be his people, and God himself will be with them; he will wipe away every tear from their eyes, and death shall be no more, neither shall there be mourning nor crying nor pain any more, for the former things have passed away. (Rev. 21:3–4.)

Or in Isaiah's magnificent vision:

> They shall not hurt or destroy
>   in all my holy mountain;
> for the earth shall be full of the knowledge
>   of the LORD
>   as the waters cover the sea.
>
> > (Isa. 11:9.)

Or in the psalmist's joyful song:

> Steadfast love and faithfulness will meet;
>   righteousness and peace will kiss
>   each other.
> Faithfulness will spring up from the ground,
>   and righteousness will look down
>   from the sky.
> Yea, the LORD will give what is good,
>   and our land will yield its increase.
> Righteousness will go before him,
>   and make his footsteps a way.
>
> > (Ps. 85:10–13.)

These are all pictures of the outcome of human life, as

God works in and with it, toward the fulfillment of his will for us. They are pictures that awaken in our hearts our deepest longings and aspirations and set before us a goal that is worth the struggle of our daily life. Indeed, no lesser purpose for this earth could really be worth what human beings go through—the work, the care, the anxiety, the pain, and the joy. This Biblical affirmation of God's goal of the Kingdom lets us realize that our labor and loves have a meaningful purpose, and that we can participate, by all we do, in a work of lasting and universal significance.

We participate in God's work in the world by obedience to his will, and that will is made clear to us through the witness of the Scriptures. God asks that we trust him for our lives and guidance and future. He asks that we look to him for all power and righteousness. He rejoices when we praise him for the life he has given us, and he bids us seek him out in worship and the word, in order that we may grow in our knowledge and trust of his working. Finally, he commands that we act toward his creation and our fellow human beings as he has acted—in love and concern, in justice and kindness, and in helping mercy. If we do these things, God promises us, we will participate in his work toward his Kingdom and we will ourselves be given an eternal place in that full and goodly realm.

How simple it all sounds, and how grievously we fall short of any fulfillment of it! We need not rehearse our separate sins to illumine the meagerness of our trust and praise, or the meanness of our mercy. We need only mentally review the history of the world's pain, product of our wars and lusts, our greeds and injustices and desperate, vain attempts to be our own gods. We creatures of God try constantly to be our own creators. We children continually run away and attempt to forget the Father.

What does the Father do? Well, he does not disown us,

nor does he leave us to our fate, orphaned and alone. He sends his Son, our elder brother, to seek us out and to find us, to tell us that the Father forgives and would like to have us come home. Indeed, the Son makes it possible for us to go home by engaging in a battle to the death all the foes who would prevent our return—fear, hatred, envy, pride, mistrust, despair, even death—all those horrible offspring spawned in our tempted and sinful hearts. Jesus Christ, by his cross and resurrection, makes it possible for us to return to the Father and thus to live the obedient life and to participate in the purpose for which God created us.

The Christian faith finds its center in the work of God in Jesus Christ, because through the mercy only there made manifest is it possible for us both to live in relation to God and to do his will. For example, on our own, apart from God, we are not very kind, but when we live in fellowship with God through Jesus Christ, we are given his power to be kind. Christian faith not only proclaims that we should do the will of God; it also gives us the power to do it. We rely daily on God's act in Jesus Christ for the gift of that power. Apart from him, as the Scripture has it, we are slaves of sin and can do nothing.

In a sense, we might say that the Christian life is lived by conducting a daily and running dialogue with the word of God, through which there is mediated to us the power and working of Jesus Christ. We read the word, or hear it preached, then apply it and find it so. Then we return and understand it further in the light of that experience. Slowly our trust and understanding grow, as we live out the word; further words take on meaning as they are illuminated in our experience, and those words are in turn lived out and allowed to shape our lives. Thus does God use our faith to shape our lives by his word and to work out the unique purpose which he has for each one of us.

Now if we have a firm and trusting grasp on these basic

affirmations of the Christian gospel, they can enable us to lay a firm foundation for our marital relations, and first of all, they can go a long way toward helping us sort out the reasons why we want to marry.

Many persons get married these days simply because it is still the socially acceptable thing to do. A surprising number of them let their friends or family push them into a union which, they are told, would "be perfect" for them. Our society still exerts subtle and terrifying pressure upon single persons to alter their unmarried status. Perhaps one of the most enlightened trends in the women's liberation movement has been its emphasis on a person's legitimate right *not* to marry, if he or she so desires. The difficulty is that the women's movement sometimes rejects marriage out of fear or even hatred. The Christian gospel, on the other hand, speaks out of a profound understanding of human freedom. It says that the direction of our lives is to be taken finally not from society's conventions and standards, but from God, who transcends every human society, and it is finally to him and him alone that we are responsible for our actions. "Do not be conformed to this world but be transformed, . . . prove what is the will of God."

There are persons, therefore, who may conscientiously decide that the will of God for them is to remain single, a practice that the Roman Catholic Church has acknowledged for centuries.[4] Certainly there can be no doubt that there are times and roles in which singleness seems an asset to the service of the purposes of God. There are times when a person can better aid his fellows without the responsibility of a family. For example, it became clear in the Confessing Church (*Bekennende Kirche*) of Germany during the Hitler era that there were risks involved for those clergy opposing the government which could not be required of married men with wives and children. The church therefore considered making it a

temporary requirement of ordination that a man promise
not to marry.[5] Even under normal circumstances, men
and women unencumbered with families can act with a
freedom from worldly concerns not possible to those with
spouse and children. Thus they can accomplish tasks
which their married colleagues cannot even undertake
(cf. I Cor. 7:32–35). Some persons are called to remain
single for the sake of the Kingdom of God, a fact not only
stated, but also exemplified, by both Jesus and Paul
(Matt. 19:10–12; I Cor. 7:7, 17, 24). God gives his own
special gift and task to both married and unmarried
(I Cor. 7:7), and finding the direction of one's life in the
will of God gives one a marvelous freedom from society's
dictates as to what one ought or ought not to do. This is
not to say that the Christian gospel makes it easier to
bear society's scorn and snickers, but it can make singleness a godly possibility.

Because the Christian gospel bestows the freedom to
choose one's course, and because it founds that freedom
on one's responsibility to God alone,[6] it also follows that
the gospel shows up inadequate reasons for marriage. It
is simply amazing why some people get married. If one
takes the trouble to read through a number of marital
case studies,[7] it becomes amply clear that persons often
doom their marital chances by the very purpose for which
they marry. Not a few, for example, enter into marriage
to legitimize sexual lust.[8] Many wed because they need
either to be dependent on a mate or, conversely, to have
power over one. In an earlier age, the perpetuation of the
family name through offspring was a legitimate reason
for wedding, just as in rural areas was the necessity of
furnishing children to work the farm. Now we do not
need more children as an economic necessity, but some
people do still marry simply because they want children.[9]
Not a few women see marriage as an escape into economic security. In the case of those formerly married,

who have children to support, some of them remarry to give another parent to their kids, or even simply because they are tired of being both parent and breadwinner. The reasons why people marry are as varied as the human condition, and many persons obviously are driven into matrimony by their slavery to their own passions or needs or wants.

Over against that slavery, the Christian gospel furnishes a kind of freedom from ourselves, a freedom to see our lives from a viewpoint that transcends our own drives and desires and puts our actions in their proper and most worthy context. We are unique creations of God, called to trust and participate in his working in our lives. In the light of that affirmation, it is possible, therefore, for us to ask: Are my reasons for wanting to marry adequate expressions of the unique purpose God has for my life? Do I believe that God wants me to share my life fully with this other person? Will I be able to use the talents he has given me in such a marriage? Will this marriage enable me to love and trust and serve God, or will it be a handicap to such devotion? Does my desire for this marriage reflect the finest desires and aspirations in me, or does it appeal to some of my more selfish and ugly moods and instincts? Can this marriage in fact have any relation to God at all? Is it my vocation, my call from God? By such examinations of one's motives over against the will of God, there can be exposed the hidden "purposes of the heart."

Few persons, however, can conduct that examination on their own. Our rationalizations and self-justifications always warp our assessments of ourselves, especially when we think we are in love. We need a Christian minister or counselor who will help us, before we get married, to uncover our particular motives for marriage and to examine them in the light of the gospel. Every Christian marriage should be preceded by expert marital *spiritual examination corresponding to physical examination.*

counseling, or by educational premarital programs within the church which have enabled us to look at ourselves truthfully, in the light of the Christian's calling. Unfortunately, far too few churches furnish such counseling or programs, but no church wedding should take place without them. If such programs are lacking, the lay people of the church should insist on them and should insist that their ministers be professionally trained to conduct them. If such programs exist in a parish, the pastor should refuse to marry any couple who has not gone through them. For far too long, many churches have spoken out of both sides of their mouths at once—condemning the breakup of the American home on the one hand, while on the other refusing to insist on that premarital counseling which could prevent scores of ill-founded and unhappy unions. The Christian gospel can give us the freedom to examine our own motives for marriage, but only if, before the wedding ceremony, it is applied.

The insights of the Christian message can also go a long way toward tempering our expectations about marriage. The wedded state has always been somewhat idealized in American society in the past, although now there are signs that that tendency is being exactly reversed. The marriage experts, David and Vera Mace, now maintain that the mass media have mounted a concerted attack on the institution of marriage, debunking it, making jokes about it, and indoctrinating the young with contempt for marriage, so that one third of the latter now see marriage as obsolete.[10] Certainly our observations of American trends tend to support the Maces' view. Yet, there is always the countertrend in American society, the "they-got-married-and lived-happily-ever-after syndrome," told about in our fairy tales, televised or otherwise, and crooned over in our popular songs, on the jukebox in the pizzeria. It is never difficult to find young persons who still believe that marriage magically solves all problems.[11]

Over against this prevalent view, the Christian faith has always maintained that marriage is not the ultimate goal of human life, that it is not, and cannot be, the be-all and end-all of existence. In the New Testament, as in the Old, marriage is a merciful gift of God, and I Tim. 4:1–5 sets forth, as an indisputable word of the Spirit, the goodness of marriage as a part of God's good creation and the judgment of God upon those who forbid marriage as evil. Yet, the New Testament views marriage as a union terminated by death (Mark 12:25 and pars.; Rom. 7:1–3; I Cor. 7:39), the implication being that the community of marriage is then replaced by the eternal, universal community of the Kingdom of God. Most radically, Jesus teaches that the demands of God are always to take precedence over the demands of marriage (Luke 14:20, 26) and family (Mark 3:31–35 and pars.; 10:29–30 and pars.; Mark 13:12 and pars.):

> He who loves father or mother more than me is not worthy of me; and he who loves son or daughter more than me is not worthy of me. (Matt. 10:37; cf. vs. 35 f.)

It is the New Testament's way of saying that the ultimate basis and meaning of our life rest in our relationship to God through Jesus Christ, and that nothing in all creation, not even God's gift of home and family, replace in importance that relationship. It really might be called a restatement of the First Commandment in relation to family life: "You shall have no other gods before me" (Ex. 20:3); marriage is not to be the object of our ultimate commitment and trust. Thus, any view of matrimony that sees in it the final fulfillment of all our needs, goals, and desires is bound to end in disillusion. God simply has not constructed the universe that way.

Similarly, the Christian affirmation of our primary responsibility to God can prevent our easy acceptance of those stereotyped roles within marriage so feared and despised by many of our young people today. Since the industrial revolution in this country and the rise of an affluent middle class, conceptions of the roles of man and wife have hardened into set expectations. The place of woman is in the home as housewife and mother, and man in the workaday world, pursuing economic security and success on behalf of his family. Despite the widespread incursion of women into the labor market and experimentations on the part of young people with alternate lifestyles, these stereotyped expectations are still very much with us.

For example, a Richmond, Virginia, newspaper reported that Jill Ruckelshaus, mother of five and wife of the former deputy attorney general of the United States, addressed a local women's club on March 5, 1975, on the necessity for women to involve themselves in politics. She apparently convinced few in her audience. One of the club members remarked pointedly after the talk, "The responsibility of the mother of five children is to those children." [12] Women's place, in the minds of many, is still very much in the home, and the concomitant of that view is the opinion, then, that women should find their satisfactions and fulfillments in the success of their husbands. The newspaper article continued:

too simple

> Another [club woman] said she thought it was common knowledge that behind every successful and good man is a successful and good woman and that in her own case, her judgment and opinion influenced her husband.

Wives, in such an opinion, are to "live through" their husbands. In the minds of many, wives really are to have no separate identity on their own.

The affirmation of the Christian faith is that each of us is created uniquely by God, with separate identities and gifts, which he expects us to use in our participation in his work in the world. Marriage, therefore, is not to mean a loss of identity, an absorption of one into another, but on the contrary, a heightening of that identity, a richer opportunity to serve God and humankind than is otherwise possible to us. God surely does not give us his merciful gift of marriage to *hinder* his purpose in the world, but to further it. Stereotyped expectations about the role of man or wife fly in the face of such purpose.

We are called in the Christian faith to a life of responsibility and trust, a life of love and forgiveness, a life of meaning and purposeful service in whatever corner of humanity God has placed us. Those who have heeded that clear call through Christ in their marriages have found, in truth, that it is precisely in their wedded relationship that they are most able to live out their Christian faith. Our love is never perfected in this world, but it is surely in relation to our mates and children that we are most able to approximate that love which Christ has for us. Our responsibility and trust are always wavering, always filled with some of our own selfishness and anxiety. Yet home and offspring enable us to exercise a responsibility toward one another, and a trust in God's good guidance, far exceeding the sense of obligation and dependence on God that we know in any other relationship. Our forgiveness is always partial, always tinged with our hurt, and yet we are most able to forgive those loved persons around our table, who have so often forgiven us.

As for meaning in life, the struggles and work of our daily round are always a mystery. That human beings should care so deeply and suffer so much, laugh and cry, speak and sing, and entertain those myriad thoughts and feelings which crowd any ordinary day, and then grow old and be no more, after all they have experienced—that is a mystery. Human life itself is a mystery that we cannot pretend to fathom fully. But when we ask what is truly good in the world, what seems most worthwhile, what turns the struggle into joy and brings closest the feeling of harmony with the purpose of God, then surely it is the love, maturing through the years of change, of a man and a woman for each other, who have learned to raise their children and to do their work and to meet life's exigencies in the mutual certitude that God holds their lives together in his hands and directs them toward his eternal and blessed outcome.

The question of whether or not to marry is finally a question about the vocation to which God has called us. It is to ask oneself, Can I better trust and obey my Lord in partnership with this other? For those who wed with that purpose informing their marital relationship, life can, for all its sorrows, be a continuing adventure in joy.

CHAPTER 3

The Committed Marriage

For this reason a man shall leave his father and mother and be joined to his wife, and the two shall become one. This is a great mystery, and I take it to mean Christ and the church.—Eph. 5:31–32

A few years ago I was involved in teaching a course at a church on the subject, "The Bible and the Modern Woman." During the term, one of the mothers in the class shared with me an excerpt from a letter written to her by her twenty-six-year-old daughter. The daughter was a college graduate, well-traveled, holding a responsible job, in love with a medical student, and deeply involved in the National Organization for Women (NOW), a women's lib group. This is the excerpt:

I feel very sure now that John [the name has been changed] is the best person for me to share my life with and he feels the same way about me. In the process of developing our relationship we have come to believe that there are means more conducive to a growing and stable relationship than that of marriage. Certainly the examples of failing marriages prevalent in our society today (e.g., John's parents) have a negative impact on any goals of marriage for us. One problem with marriage is that it eliminates many options that are necessary for individuals fully to mature—by way of its legal, economic and social "requirements." An obvious example to me is that a woman, married, is considered even less of a whole person in the eyes of the law than a single woman (who is about ¾ a person these days!).

So John and I propose to live together for a year to give us time to work out our domestic roles and get a better idea of each other's life goals to be further sure that they can be shared and/or coexist. As you know, I am not interested in the housewife position even though it may bring satisfaction to some women. I want to finish my higher degree for one thing. John still has many questions about his commitment to his profession. . . .

Each year since college, the idea of marriage as the best and *only* way of having a full life has become less significant to me. We each have had several close relationships and do not feel now as much the need for the security of marriage in order to have one. The options are more easily available by not being married and we believe can contribute to fuller communication. At this stage of our relationship, living together will be a big enough step. For people to change and grow they must be part of an open system and not one that becomes locked in, which is much more likely to happen in marriage. In time we hope our relationship will grow sufficiently to be strong enough to include the external bond of marriage in a long-term commitment that would include having children.

If we find that there are just too many hassles trying to live decently under this proposal (such as renting an apartment, keeping my job or getting a new one), I'm sure we would get married. You can be sure we have no intention of being martyrs just to make a point. The important thing is that marriage is not our first choice, according to our idealistic view of what contributes best to a growing relationship, but nevertheless, it is a strong second choice. I've grown a lot in the past few years with the help of the women's liberation movement and through my job, but I realize I have much more to learn. I'm still idealistic about a lot of things and

hope to maintain and increase the ability to carry out my
convictions. In essence we both probably are taking the
marriage decision *too* seriously rather than not seriously
enough.

This is an excellent example of what is happening to
the institution of marriage today. Young persons are
rejecting static understandings and stereotyped roles in
marriage. They are looking for deeply intimate relationships with their life partners, in which they can together
share life goals and work. In this daughter's mind, the
traditional institution of marriage "eliminates many options that are necessary for individuals fully to mature,"
and "there are means more conducive to a growing and
stable relationship than that of marriage." In the traditional marriage, one "becomes locked in," whereas "for
people to change and grow they must be part of an open
system"; "options" must be held open. In short, this
young woman wants to grow and mature as a human
being, and she is quite sure that it is impossible to do so
within the confines of marriage as it is usually understood
in our culture.

Certainly from a Christian point of view, we can only
applaud this daughter's desire to cultivate a dynamic and
intimate relationship with her life's partner. Because
marriage has for so long been viewed as an institution,
with set roles for husband and wife, there have developed
patterns of married life in the United States which are far
from desirable. In far too many households, spouses live
largely separate lives, fulfilling their expected roles to be
sure, and yet each pursuing his or her separate interests,
sharing almost no time or concerns, and actually remaining strangers to each other, simply happening to
inhabit the same living quarters.

In other marriages, husband or wife has been almost
totally depersonalized and turned into a service machine,
programmed to achieve material success or status for the
family. Some husbands almost—and sometimes literally!

—kill themselves on their jobs, in order that their wives may have the clothes, money, and social standing which belong to the American upper class. Other times it is the wife who is victimized, constantly on demand as a hostess to further her husband's business contacts. For example, in a booklet prepared by the Alexander Hamilton Institute of New York, written by Faye Henle and entitled *The Executive's Wife,* wives of rising young executives were given these pieces of advice:

> Accept the fact that your husband is no longer an 8-hours-a-day worker . . . [his] company becomes part of your family's success story. . . . Your personality and appearance may have a great deal to do with your husband's fortunes in the business world. . . . This means constant attention to diet, grooming, wardrobe and manner of dealing with people. . . . Your home needn't be a palace, but you may have to learn to run it royally . . . entertaining business associates. . . .
>
> Don't resent these extra demands on your time and services. Your husband is working under more of a strain, and as his life's partner, his goal is your goal. If you like the prospect of his bringing home more money . . . moving you and the family to a nicer neighborhood . . . fancier schools, clothes and vacations—you'd better pitch in. Without complaining!
>
> It takes a lot of inner strength and chin-up routine to smile when your husband misses dinner and seeing the kids before bedtime several nights a week. It's even harder when he packs a bag and jets into the wild blue yonder. . . . Keep happy with the thought that this sacrifice of your husband's helping hands around the house may one day release both of you from . . . chores forever. Any worthwhile goal is going to demand payment in advance. So bear up! [13]

Thus has the great god of "success" taken over innumerable American marriages. We can only hope that our current crop of young people, in their desire for companionship in their marriages, have left behind forever such depersonalized and materialistic slavery.

The difficulty is, however, that many young persons

such as the daughter whose letter was quoted above, have come to the conclusion that in order to grow and mature as human beings and in order to have a completely sharing relationship, marriage must be avoided altogether. Precisely by that conclusion, such young people have made an intimate and joyful lifelong relationship with one another almost impossible to achieve.

The marital relationship of lifelong companionship is founded on total commitment. This is one of the reasons why the author of the letter to the Ephesians has compared marriage to the relation of Christ with his church (Eph. 5:31–32). Christ has totally committed himself to his community of followers. He has promised to be with us always (Matt. 28:20). He has made us as his own body (I Cor. 12:27; Eph. 5:28–30). He has loved us even when we have been unfaithful, and he has poured out his life for us, not hesitating even to die for us in order that we may live.

That commitment by our Lord Jesus Christ shows us the meaning of love. Indeed, if we were to take the famous passage on love in I Cor., ch. 13, and substitute the word "Christ" for the word "love" in it, the meaning would be the same:

> Christ is patient and kind; Christ is not jealous or boastful; he is not arrogant or rude. Christ does not insist on his own way; he is not irritable or resentful; he does not rejoice at wrong, but rejoices in the right. Christ bears all things, believes all things, hopes all things, endures all things. Christ never ends. (I Cor. 13:4–8.)

It is that kind of love—the love that Christ has had for us—that we are to have for one another in our marriages: "This is my commandment, that you love one another as I have loved you" (John 15:12). We often ask what it means to love God, and how we can live out that love. God answers us by giving us the command to love our neighbor (cf. I John 4:7–21), the nearest and dearest of whom is the mate with whom we live. "We love, because he first loved us." (I John 4:19.) With the love with which he has loved us, we are to love our marital partners.

The primary characteristic of the love of Christ is that he has poured out himself for us. He has committed himself totally to us, to be with us in life and death. It is that kind of commitment upon which Christian marriage is to be founded. It is love that gives itself away, love that always cares about what happens to us, love that wills only good for us and wants us to have life abundant, love that constantly works to bring about that good. With that loving commitment to be with and to work for the good of the other, we are to commit ourselves in our marriages. As the beginning of Eph., ch. 5, puts it: "Therefore be imitators of God, as beloved children. And walk in love, as Christ loved us and gave himself up for us"—total and unstinting commitment.

Up against that kind of pattern for our marriage unions, it is clear what mistake the daughter quoted above is making in trying to build a relationship with her man: she is refusing to commit herself totally to him. To be sure, she wants the right things: a living, dynamic companionship of total sharing with the one she loves. She reflects very accurately our depersonalized, bureaucratized, rootless, fast-moving, pressurized culture's longing for meaningful and intimate personal relationships. She cries out, with the women's movement's cry, for the chance to be a whole, loving human being. But she omits from her actions the one element that might make her goals realizable: total and noncalculating commitment to her man.

Instead, the daughter wants to hold her options open, try out the marital relationship, see if it works, experiment for a year with a "trial marriage." By that lack of commitment, she has almost inevitably doomed her relationship to failure. Statistical psychological and sociological studies have confirmed that most so-called "trial marriages" in this country end in the separation of the partners. It could almost be said that if one wants to ensure that a subsequent marital relationship will fail, then one should "try it out" for a year before entering into it. Marital relations in which commitment to the union is lacking scarcely ever have a chance.

Many of the young persons entering into trial marriages maintain that they really do have a commitment to one another and that they therefore do not need the formality and legalism of a marriage license and ceremony, which they see as meaningless and inhibiting conventions. The truth is that they have not made a lasting commitment to one another at all. As with the daughter above, they are still holding open their options. Given the conflicts that always arise in intimate relationships, it is almost certain that the partners to the trial marriage will part and embark once again on an uncommitted and therefore vain search for other mates with whom they think they will be more "compatible."

Just the fact that such young people are hesitant legally to seal their union is evidence that their commitment to one another is not total. Marriage licenses and ceremonies are not only legal formalities; they are also symbols of responsibility. They say publicly, what is affirmed privately, without reservation, that I am responsible for my mate—responsible not only in all those lovely emotional and spiritual areas of married life, but responsible also in the down-to-earth areas that have to do with grubby things like money, health insurance, and property. For example, two people just living together have no obligation for each other when the tax form comes up for an audit, or the other is involved in a car accident and legal suit; but persons holding a marriage license do have such responsibility, and commitment to a marriage involves accepting that public responsibility too. It is a matter of accepting the full obligations that society imposes on its adult members in order to ensure the common good.

So Christian marriage is *committed marriage*. That is its basic characteristic. And that commitment is to be *total commitment*, an unreserved dedication of one's whole self to the relationship. When Christians marry, they say to each other, in effect, "We are going to maintain this marital union, no matter what." It is this unreserved dedication to the union which the Christian marriage vows set forth: "for better for worse, for richer for poorer, in sickness and in health." That is, Christian mates promise to each other: "I will be with you, no matter what happens to us and between us. If you should become blind tomorrow, I will be there. If you achieve no success and attain no status in our society, I will be there. When we argue and are angry, as we inevitably will, I will work to bring us together. When we seem totally at odds and neither of us is having needs fulfilled, I will persist in trying to understand and in trying to restore our relationship. When our marriage seems utterly sterile and going nowhere at all, I will believe that it can work and I will want it to work, and I will do my part to make it work. And when all is wonderful and we are happy, I will rejoice over our life together, and continue to strive to keep our relationship growing and strong." Christ promised us, "I am with you always, even to the end of the age." Christians, in marriage, take upon themselves that same unreserved commitment.

The question inevitably arises, Is such a total commitment possible? Or are we Christians in our marriage vows being naive and foolish, and promising to each other a lifelong love that we cannot possibly deliver? Would it not be better to go with the modern version of the marriage vow, and state that we shall remain together "as long as we both shall love"?

Certainly a lot of persons in American society would answer such questions in the affirmative. No one, they believe, can possibly make a total commitment to another person, and to think we can is to kid ourselves about the realities of human life. We had better face up, the cynics say, to the fragility of the marriage bond, and not expect superhuman faithfulness from weak and imperfect human nature. Christ may have committed himself totally to his church, but he was perfect. We are not, and we had better realize the fact.

Even marriage counselors have their doubts about the Christian wedding vows. Says Carl Rogers, "The value of such outward commitment appears to me to be just about nil." [14]

The answer to that is that thousands of persons have so committed themselves in Christian marriage and have achieved lifelong unions amazing in their tenderness and persistent in their devotion to the end. Nor should we think that such healthy marriages are simply the product of fantastic luck—that the partners have been fortunate enough to find persons with whom they could be happy.

Over against all skepticism about the possibility of Christian marital happiness, the church can affirm from centuries of experience that the Christian faith is not a fairy tale. When Christ promises abundant life to those who trust him and rely on his power and guidance, he gives us a sure promise on which we can count—although every true Christian knows that abundant life and life free from trouble and suffering are not synonymous. But there is a wholeness, and joy, peace, and goodness that are given to those who are faithful, and these are gifts that are given also to those who are faithful to their marital commitments.

God works within Christian marriages—that is the unseen factor which the marriage manuals so often ignore. He lends Christian couples his power through Christ to hold fast their commitment. God is indeed a rock and a fortress and a sure defender, as the Scriptures say he is. Marriages built on him do not crumble as easily as those built upon the sand of human loyalty.

Nevertheless, Christian couples are not relieved of their responsibility for working to maintain and deepen their unions. As the apostle Paul put it so perceptively, even our salvation is both a gift and a response: "Work out your own salvation with fear and trembling; for God is at work in you, both to will and to work for his good pleasure" (Phil. 2:12–13). We have strenuously to achieve our own marital happiness, and yet God is at work in and through and even beyond our efforts to give us abundant life together. God alone gives life, but it is our responsibility to achieve it; we achieve successful marriages, and yet they are solely the gift of God. Such is the paradox which every happily married Christian couple know to be profoundly true.

We therefore have something else to do in Christian marriage. We must also learn to accept each other, with all our faults and imperfections. Christian marriage is not only total commitment; it is also *accepting commitment,* learning to love and value the other for the imperfect person he or she is. Young lovers may think each other perfect before they wed, but reality soon asserts itself. Every married person puts up with a number of traits and actions on the part of a mate which are disagreeable and sometimes embarrassing. To be sure, there are some things that can wreck a marriage—alcoholism, neurotic or psychotic fears and demands, infidelity, mental or physical cruelty. Those evils belong in a class by themselves and must be treated separately. But in the typical, everyday Christian marriage, there are lots of petty irritations and dislikes, and the committed marriage is one in which we learn to accept, in love, the other's imperfections.

Probably the most marvelous thing about a committed marriage is that it is totally a relationship of grace, a relationship in which a person does not have to earn or deserve love, but in which love is always given. There is no more freeing realization that a human being can have than to realize that he or she may grievously err and yet be cared for, accepted, and loved as a lovable and valuable human being.

It is precisely for this reason that the Christian faith says that Jesus Christ gives us freedom—because in his sight we always fall short or go astray and yet are always loved and valued. "While we were yet sinners Christ died for us" (Rom. 5:8)—we did not have to earn his love! Wander as we will into that "far country" of fault or profligacy, the Father welcomes us home (Luke 15:11–32)!

So it is in the committed marriage—I do not have to earn my mate's love. He gives it to me as a gift, in a sheer act of grace. In fact, I could not earn or deserve such love, any more than I can earn or deserve the love of Christ. Love is never deserved, because most of the time, we are not very lovable. Yet love is given to me; I am cared for and cherished in a mysterious miracle beyond my fathoming, and that gives me the freedom to act and to be me, as nothing else does.

It is the mystery of love in marriage that commitment leads to freedom—freedom to move out from a sure base of security and acceptance, freedom to plumb all my creativity, freedom to be my authentic self much more than if I did not have such security. Jesus told us in his teaching, "Whoever would save his life will lose it; and whoever loses his life for my sake, he will save it" (Luke 9:24 and pars.). The truth of that teaching becomes abundantly clear in the relationship of marriage. When we commit ourselves, when we give ourselves to each other in the relation of matrimony, when we lose ourselves in a total and accepting dedication to the other, then we most surely find our freedom to be ourselves, then we most fully discover that we can live and love.

Christian marriage is also characterized by an *exclusive commitment* to the other—as the Christian marriage vows put it, "to forsake all others" and "to keep thee only unto her [or him], so long as ye both shall live." [15] That has seemed an outdated legalism to many in our swinging society. In an age when our young people have lost many of the Victorian attitudes toward sex and see it as a natural expression of caring, experimentation with open sex or group sex is a widespread phenomenon.

We must distinguish carefully between various forms of sexual experimentation however. There are, in every age, those who play games with sex—who use it to exploit, to gain power, or to manipulate other people. The fictional James Bond or the playboy Hugh Heffner comes immediately to mind as examples, and despite the public attention they receive, they have nothing good to offer marriage. But there are also many young persons in this country for whom sex is not a game at all, but a sincere expression of affection and caring for other persons. With their skeptical views about traditional marriage, these young persons have experimented rather widely with free and open sex in marriage and out of marriage, and the results of these experiments are now being systematically studied by marriage counselors.[16]

Counselors, wholly sympathetic to such experimentation, have been surprised with the results. Let me quote some lines from Carl Rogers, who has studied commune life rather closely:

> . . . one of the elemental facts about many communes is that they are experimental laboratories where—without guilt, without public knowledge outside of the group, without a commitment to any one mode of behavior—a variety of sexual unions can be tried. What is, for many people, a fantasied variety of sexual experiences is here brought alive in reality.
>
> But all of this experimentation is not without cost. The sense of loss, of hurt, of jealousy, of self-pity, of anger, of

desire for retaliation are experienced time and time again by those involved in the experimentation. No matter how "modern" the person's point of view, or his or her intellectual commitment, someone is hurt in one way or another . . . every time partnerships shift. And jealousy does not necessarily relate simply to sexual behavior, but to such things as a loss of closeness.[17]

From this, Rogers draws two interesting conclusions:

Jealousy is often an underestimated problem which can undermine a group. Indeed, I wonder whether jealousy is something simply conditioned by the culture or actually has a basic biological foundation, like territoriality.

Related to this is, I believe, a similar underestimation of the need of each person for a reasonably secure, continuing, one-to-one relationship. This need seems to run very deep and may be considered too lightly.[18]

David and Vera Mace, in their studies, have reached a similar conclusion:

This need for a one-to-one relationship in which we give ourselves, and find ourselves, through total sharing with another seems to be a widespread and fundamental human need.[19]

In short, actual case studies are showing that the exclusive commitment of Christian marriage is not merely the product of straitlaced and earlier times, but a deep, abiding need which human beings have built into their constitution by their Creator. Apparently when God commanded, "You shall not commit adultery" (Ex. 20:14), he was making wise and loving provision for our ultimate happiness!

It must also be noted that the exclusive commitment of Christian marriage is not limited to the sexual sphere, a fact that wives sometimes are more quick to sense than are their husbands. The latter sometimes feel that they

can enter into an intimate relation with another woman,
so long as that intimacy is not expressed sexually. But
women seem instinctively to know that marital commitment can also be violated by the intrusion of other closer
emotional ties—though some women too have violated
their marriages by forming relationships with friends or
relatives closer than those with their husbands. It is
difficult to give oneself away totally to more than one
person. We apparently each need the security and the
resultant freedom that come from total commitment to
one other human being, and the fullest and most satisfying expression of that commitment is certainly the marital union, with its total involvement of the personality:
mind, body, and spirit.

The commitment of a Christian marriage is also a
continuing commitment, a commitment that is never
made simply once and for all. The young man who asked
his fiancée if she would still love him when he was bald
and fat was more realistic than he knew. Time changes
all things, including the persons we are, and marital
commitment must continue through the changes. We
pass through the seasons of life—the zest of youth with
its beginnings of home, family, and job; the multitudinous
activities of parenthood when every minute is taken; the
middle years, with kids in college and parents old and
dying, when suddenly life seems all too short and dreams
have not been realized; the decline of physical vigor and
the entrance into retirement, and then all so quickly the
label of "senior citizen" and intimations of the end. In
each season, with each change, the marital commitment
must be made anew. Like love for God, it is never
accomplished once and for all, but only for the day that
lies immediately at hand.

Indeed, it may be said that the Christian commitment
to marriage, like love and trust in God, is a commitment
that is acted out in every day's activities. It must be

affirmed when one's mate gets out of bed grumpy in the morning, when decisions are made about the day's activities, when money is spent, or the kids are disciplined, or plans for the future are laid. It must be made when we are tired or zestful, when we are happy or in sorrow. It must be made in the middle of quarrels and when all is going well. In all life's seasons, and in all life's moods, we decide for or against our marriage, not only by what we think and feel but also by what we do. There, in the stuff of life, we make or break commitment. To enter into the Christian marriage commitment is to take on a lifelong task, which never ends until in fact, death does us part.

Most important, Christian marital commitment is a *growing commitment,* which matures and deepens as time and life multiply our experiences.

There is certainly an initial maturity which a person must have before he or she can enter Christian marriage. Those who are not whole persons in their own right, who are still dependent for their security and satisfactions on their parents, or who are seeking only the gratification of their own psychological or sexual needs, or who are looking for someone to take care of them emotionally and physically, obviously cannot even initially commit themselves to the self-expenditure of work and caring which Christian marriage requires. Those who desire to rule over or manipulate another person in order to bolster their own self-esteem or to foster their own sense of power and worth cannot commit themselves to the self-sacrifice and sharing that Christian marriage demands. Christ's love for his church, which is the pattern for marriage, is the love of a whole and mature person. Our love in Christian marriage is possible only in the same maturity.

Such maturity is not achieved overnight. Usually it itself is the product of a healthy home life. The ability to share with another, to care for another's needs, to sacrifice one's own wants for the good of another, the ability to accept responsibility and to exercise one's talents, and to maintain one's own self-esteem—all of these usually are the gifts passed on to us by our own parents, and all of them are indispensable requirements for entering matrimony. There must be a basic health of personality before marriage is even contemplated.

Then, given that basic health, there is a growth that must take place within our marriages, a maturing and deepening of our love and commitment to our mates. It has always been recognized in the Christian life that we are to grow in "sanctification"—as Ephesians puts it, that we are to grow up "to the measure of the stature of the fulness of Christ" (Eph. 4:13), until we love with the fullness of his love. The necessity for that growth includes the sphere of our marriages. There is to be a maturing and deepening of our love and commitment to each other.

To give only one example, in the initial months of every marriage, the new husband and wife must learn what it means to be "we" instead of separate "I" 's. That is not always an easy task. Other males and females must now be related to differently than they were before. Parents and ties to home must be seen in a new light. Claims on time and affection between the new partners must be understood and adjusted. Unsuspected flaws in each one's personality come to light and must be accepted. All sorts of modifications in relations with friends and relatives and each other and one's self have to be made, and the initial marital commitment of the couple has to grow to accommodate those modifications. So it is all through the marriage. Commitment has to grow and mature in order to accommodate life's changes.

The sad fact is, however, that most marriages do not grow in maturity and love. Instead, they wither. Marriage experts have found that most American husbands and wives perceive their marriages to be less and less satisfactory over the passing years.[20] That means that the marital partners have not learned to adjust their commitment to life's changes, have not learned to persist and mature in their relationship with each other through the passing years. Energy has not been expended to keep the relationship improving, intimacies have not been strengthened, hostilities have not been resolved. Instead, the partners have either settled down into an accustomed routine with each other, in which nothing new is expected—though much new is taking place—or mutual hostilities have hardened into habits and the partners have become resigned to them. There is nothing more disheartening than to see a marriage that has ossified, in which all has become dull routine. And nothing is more tragic than to watch the partners in such a stultified relationship searching outside of their relationship for someone or something to give them some excitement and sense of growth. When we stop growing in this life, we begin to die, and marital commitment that stops deepening and widening begins to wither away.

For this reason, marriage experts are now talking more and more about "marriage enrichment," about group discussions and exercises in which average couples can come together to help one another grow and realize new possibilities in their marriages. David and Vera Mace have begun a nationwide organization called ACME (Association of Couples for Marriage Enrichment, 403 S. Hawthorne Road, Winston-Salem, N.C. 27103) precisely for this purpose. Many larger churches are now beginning to set up such programs.

To undergird such efforts, perhaps what we also need on the part of Christian married couples is a renewed awareness of that Biblical perception of the lively action of God in our lives. It is the affirmation of Christian faith that God has a purpose for each of our lives and that he is working in us and through us and with us, fulfilling that purpose. Given that fact, how then can any one of us expect our mate to remain the same person? God is working with him or her, shaping his or her life in new ways through new experiences. Should we not be open in our relationship with our mates to be surprised by that working, to find that he or she is being led into new thoughts and experiences? God is leading my spouse, and leading me with him, working out his marvelous plan for our marriage together. Should I not then anticipate unexpected outcomes, new paths and new ways down which God leads our life together? Certainly as I look back over our marriage, that has been the case. As I face the future, I am equally sure that there will be further surprises. Perhaps we Christian married couples, then, should bring an *anticipating commitment* to our marriages, a commitment which anticipates that God has much yet to do with us. As I John puts it so marvelously with that eager anticipation of the future: "Beloved, we are God's children now; it does not yet appear what we shall be" (I John 3:2).

There is risk in the Christian marital commitment, the risk of total vulnerability. As with our Lord, when we give ourselves away in love, the result may be a crucifixion. But there is no other gateway into the joys of a Christian marriage. To know the good life in marriage which God intended for us to know, we must commit ourselves in unreserved devotion. When our devotion is received and answered, when our mate responds with like affection, then the heights and depths of the resulting relationship is, like life itself, a mystery that we can only receive from God in utter gratitude and joy—the mystery of two persons become one flesh, the mystery of two lives proceeding together, separate yet profoundly joined, in a continuing and growing communion.

CHAPTER 4

Marriage in a Revolutionary Time

For men will be lovers of self, . . . holding the form of religion but denying the power of it. Avoid such people. For among them are those who make their way into households and capture weak women, burdened with sins and swayed by various impulses, who will listen to anybody and can never arrive at a knowledge of the truth. . . . But as for you, continue in what you have learned and have firmly believed, knowing from whom you learned it and how from childhood you have been acquainted with the sacred writings which are able to instruct you for salvation through faith in Christ Jesus.

—II Tim. 3:2, 5–7, 14–15

No discussion of marriage and family life today dare ignore the women's liberation movement. We are undergoing a quiet revolution in the United States, in which the basic structures of our society are being drastically altered. Marriage as an institution, with a dominant role for the man and a subservient role for the wife, is dying out and being replaced by the companionship marriage between two fully equal partners. Educators and the mass media are being forced to project new images of the activities and aspirations of male and female. Government is gradually affording women more opportunities. Economic life is slowly accommodating to the permanent presence of women in the labor force, and the "success syndrome" for men is being called, at least by some, into question. Child rearing more and more must adjust to the absence of both parents from the home. Even our language is being restructured to acknowledge the full personhood of women, as all the awkward he or she and him or her pronouns in this book attest. To say that all of these changes are having an enormous effect on the American home has become a truism that no knowledgeable person would dispute. The husband and wife who face each other across the breakfast table in this decade are radically different individuals from the spouses in a similar situation even ten or fifteen years ago.

Women's movements are over a century old in the United States. The first substantial women's rights movement had its birth in the abolitionist cause preceding the Civil War, when women who set out to plead for the rights of slaves found themselves barred from conventions and speaker's platforms. When females won the right to vote in 1920, with the passage of the Nineteenth Amendment to the Constitution, the struggle for women's rights largely died out and for a time was forgotten.

It was not until the 1960's that the battle was renewed. At that time, two distinct branches of the feminist movement arose and have been active ever since.

The first was spawned by the publication, in 1963, of Betty Friedan's book, *The Feminine Mystique.* It was the author's thesis in that book that American women were being cruelly deceived by a feminine mystique or stereotype. During World War II, said Friedan, women out of necessity and in large numbers entered into the labor market and were afforded an important place in the country's industrial structure. However, as soon as the war was over, women were urged by advertising and a consumer-oriented society to return to their homes, to find their creativity and satisfactions in homemaking, and to confine their efforts to a stereotyped role as housekeepers, wives, and mothers. The result of this, maintained Friedan, was that women were no longer able to grow to their full capacity as persons, but were drowning in detergent suds, trying to bolster their egos by floorwaxing, and unhappily asking themselves, "Who am I?" and "Is this all?" This, wrote Friedan, was "the problem without a name" and it was typical of most middle-class females.

Apparently the Friedan book struck a responsive chord in American females, for despite widespread ridicule, it became an instant best seller. It spawned the National Organization for Women, and led to nationwide efforts on the part of women to gain new opportunities in education, employment, government, and society at large. Indeed, it may be said that this moderate branch of the women's movement has mushroomed into a consciousness on the part of women throughout the nation of their need for equal roles and personhood. It is doubtful that the effects of this movement will ever again be reversed in American society.

The other branch of the modern feminist movement in the United States is entirely different in origin. It is the radical wing, which is made up largely of young, middle-class white women who got their start in the civil rights movement and in the college branches of the New Left. As *Newsweek* magazine put it, these women learned in the civil rights struggle what it was like "to have a college education and to be offered a porter's job. Their contributions seldom were allowed to go beyond sweeping floors, making coffee, typing stencils and bedding down," [21] inferior positions typified by the remark of Stokely Carmichael, who maintained that the only position for a woman in SNCC was prone. Such treatment bred a deep sense of resentment in these women, and in mid-1967, starting with a meeting in Chicago, they began organizing their own groups to fight for their rights. Their organizations and publications are multitudinous, and they form no nationwide, united group. It is in this radical wing of the feminist movement that one finds the militants, the bra burners, the men haters.

For example, Roxanne Dunbar, a leader in Boston and later Louisiana, stated:

> We do not ignore what seem to be the "petty" forms of our oppression, such as total identification with housework and sexuality as well as physical helplessness. Rather we understand that our oppression and suppression are institutionalized, that all women suffer the "petty" forms of oppression. Therefore they are not petty or personal, but rather constitute a widespread, deeply rooted social disease. They are the things that keep us tied down day to day, and do not allow us to act. Further, we understand that all men are our policemen, and no organized police force is necessary to keep us in our places. All men enjoy male supremacy and take advantage of it to a greater or lesser degree, according to their own hierarchy of power.[22]

Dunbar therefore advocated a total restructuring of society on Marxist models. Men, she said, have ruined society, with their masculine values of competition and violence, and feminine values of cooperation with nature and each other must be restored. If they are, then the good society will be one in which the decadent institution of the family will be destroyed, all housework will be industrialized, the public education and care of children will begin at birth, men will share in the responsibilities of maternal care and consciousness, and women will be free to form a community of work, as equals with men. In addition, it was Dunbar who was the first "publicly to advocate masturbation as an alternative to what she sees as the slavery of heterosexuality" [23] and it is among like radicals that homosexuality has been widely touted as a legitimate alternative to male-female sexual relations.

Such extremism has evoked extensive criticism of the women's movement, not only among the general public but also from the scientific community. Dr. Abram Kardiner, former head of psychiatry at Columbia University, stated: "From what I've seen of the liberationists, their most conspicuous feature is self-hatred. I see tremendous vituperativeness and lack of feeling. They think it's a curse to be female and have exaggerated opinions about the merits of being a male." [24]

Moderates such as Friedan or Simone de Beauvoir have specifically rejected the radicals' hatred of men. "Man," wrote Friedan, "is not the enemy, but the fellow victim of the present half-equality," [25] because men not only suffer from having wives who are stunted in their personal growth, but also bear the burden of having constantly to compete in our consumer-oriented society to furnish those wives with more and more things and gadgets and beauty aids to shore up their artificial roles. It is a fantasy deviation, according to Friedan, to talk about a society in which there is no love, no sex, no marriage: "We have to deal with the world of reality if we are going to have a real revolution." [26]

A real revolution is exactly what the moderates have spawned, and according to the polls, American women are increasingly in favor of efforts to improve their status. For example, in a 1970 Roper poll, only 40 percent of American women approved such efforts; in 1974, the percentage rose to 57 percent. Surprisingly, too, 63 percent of the men polled in 1974 approved the women's egalitarian efforts. With respect to marriage, 46 percent of the women surveyed preferred a marriage "where husband and wife share responsibilities more—both work, both share homemaking and child responsibilities," and 52 percent of the women questioned said they wanted to combine a career with marriage and raising children.[27] Old conceptions of marriage roles and women's place have succumbed to new views of men and women.

Similarly, the old arguments against women's full participation in society have been shown to be largely unfounded. There used to be the constant criticism that working wives contribute to juvenile delinquency and that they therefore ought to stay at home with their children. But psychological studies have consistently failed to show that working mothers have more delinquent children. Psychologists have frequently pointed out that the woman who finds personal satisfaction in a job often brings into her family a happiness and stimulation unknown to the wife who is restless at home, though admittedly such arguments have usually failed to convince those who are certain that woman's place is in the home.

Sometimes it has been maintained that women contribute to unemployment for men and keep wage scales down. However, 35 million American women are now in the labor force, and it is recognized by all economists that they are absolutely essential there. As early as 1958, the chairman of the National Manpower Council stated: "The answer to the question—what would happen if all working wives would give up their jobs?—is that the economy would collapse and that we would not be able to perform the essential services needed. It would be a disaster of incredible magnitude." [28] Or as economist Sylvia Porter put it, "our economy would grind to a halt in a matter of hours." [29]

Others have argued that woman was intended to be only a homemaker because that is her universal role throughout the world. But modern anthropology has shown that no such generalizations are valid. In some cultures, it is the woman who works in the fields or hunts or engages in warfare, while the man tends to home tasks and the raising of children. Some cultures regard those tasks which we call "feminine" as predominantly "masculine," and variations on the roles of man and woman are almost as numerous as societies themselves. Anthropologist Margaret Mead believes that many traits we call masculine and feminine are inherited stereotypes and proposes that men share child-rearing and domestic chores and that women be encouraged to learn aggressive, masculine pursuits.[30]

Nor are women intended to be only homemakers because they are biologically built that way. Psychologists who have tested femininity and masculinity to find their relation to biological characteristics, "have shown that, while men seem to excel in certain areas and to have certain characteristics and women others, the differences are not very clearly defined, and the differences between individuals in each sex are greater than between the sexes as a whole. We have come to realize that each of us has within himself both masculine and feminine qualities in varying proportions, and that these are needed for a healthy and well-rounded personality."[31] Thus have scientific studies shown the fallacies of familiar arguments against woman's participation in society.

Yet, stereotypes die slowly, and our economy, our educational facilities, our laws, still favor limiting woman's role to that of homemaker and mother. As recently as February 1975, economist Sylvia Porter was forced to write a blistering column against a fellow newspaperman who maintained that women did not *need* to work and therefore should drop out of the labor market to ease unemployment. Porter pointed out in rebuttal that of the 35 million women employed, 7 million are single and must support themselves or others; 6,300,000 are widowed, divorced, or separated and work for compelling economic reasons; 3.7 million add to their husbands' sub-$5,000 annual incomes; one million are their family's sole support; and about 2.6 million contribute half or more of the family's income—indisputable evidence that women work out of economic need and, as the Department of Labor's Employment Standards Division put it, "for the same reasons men do." [32]

Although educational institutions are scrambling to hire more women in order to qualify for federal aid, full professors and department chairmen still are usually men, and the bulk of academic women are associated with low-status or low-prestige institutions, such as teachers colleges and junior colleges. Women are increasingly being admitted into graduate and professional schools, but they still must cope with residency requirements and the lack of day care centers for their children.

In financial life, women still have difficulty qualifying for consumer credit, insurance, and mortgages. Under the government health insurance policies, it costs a woman $2.80 per month more to cover herself and her husband than it would cost a male to cover himself, his wife, and two small children.[33] Under the Social Security law, working wives receive almost no equity at all. According to that tax law, working wives pay into Social Security on the same basis as their working husbands, but when they retire, they cannot necessarily draw on what they have paid in. Instead they must decide whether to draw benefits as working women or wives. If both husband and wife have worked at fairly low incomes, which is frequently the case (6.7 million working wives have husbands with annual incomes of less than $7,000), the fact is that while they have paid as much or more in social security taxes than the man who was the sole family earner and paid at the top base, they will nevertheless draw less than the amount going to that man and his non-earning wife. To correct this unfair tax burden on married working couples would have cost more than two billion dollars six years ago. It would cost untold billions now—evidence of the extent to which the working wife has unfairly been forced to subsidize Social Security.[34]

There is no doubt that there is still discrimination against women in American society, and most of the basic structures of our society are designed to limit woman's role to her home. The difficulty is, however, that our homes have drastically changed in the twentieth century, and many women no longer find homemaking a task that challenges them sufficiently.

It used to be that our homes were rural producing communities, turning out clothes, food, and marketable products. Such is no longer the case. We no longer create the necessities of life within our homes. We merely consume them, which means that much of the purposive activity that formerly occupied the housewife —gardening, canning, sewing, quilting, baking, keeping chickens—has now become merely a hobby or has been abandoned altogether. The modern housewife really has little *necessary* creative activity left to her in her home. She must of necessity carry out only the rather dull routines of washing and ironing, cleaning and arranging, preparing and serving food, and even many of the tasks involved in those routines are done by someone else: the local laundry, the bakery delivery service, the frozen food providers. To be sure, the modern housewife could give up her clothes drier, bake all her own bread, and make the clothing for the entire family, but that is really not the kind of world we live in. Sooner or later she would become convinced that she was wasting time. She needs purposive activity that fully engages her energies and interests, and she often now seeks this outside of her household.

Because of the mobility of modern society, families are also increasingly isolated. The wife who follows her husband from job to job is usually cut off from her relatives, and she very often lives in a succession of neighborhoods as an almost complete stranger. She obviously needs human companionship, but often her only company for most of the day are her small children or, after they are in school, perhaps a neighbor or two. She therefore longs to get out in the world where she can talk to someone—anyone—on an adult level and where she can experience that discussion and conflict by which alone her thinking grows.

In addition, it must be realized that the modern woman frequently is educated. Since she has studied international relations or modern physics right along with men, she really cannot be blamed for finding her role as a housewife somewhat limiting. Some persons have actually suggested that since modern education makes women restless, perhaps the solution to the problem would be not to educate them, or rather to give them only those courses which would prepare them as housewives and mothers. This too is a solution that belongs to an age forever gone.

The modern American woman wishes to grow, to be engaged in some meaningful and demanding activity on her own. She has no desire to compete with her husband, and she certainly does not want to give up her home and family. She finds her major satisfactions in her role as a wife and mother, and she would exchange that role for nothing else and no one. In a Roper poll, nine out of ten women surveyed preferred marriage over all other alternative life-styles. At the same time, the American female wants her personhood stretched to its full measure. At home she often feels that she is merely "vegetating," and that the simple tasks of running a household present her with no real challenge to which she can rise, no demand that necessitates personal and intellectual growth. To quote psychiatrist Joseph Noshpitz:

> Our minds, our intelligence, our emotions, our characters grow, by being frustrated. We grow, psychologically, by encountering a difficulty, and mastering it. We grow by solving problems. We don't grow by stagnating, or by avoiding difficulties, or by just being.[35]

For this reason, American females are increasingly turning to activities outside their homes. Some of them are engaged in community charity and social projects, although they confess that such activities often furnish them with little sense of lasting purpose. Some have found deep and stimulating satisfactions from cultural or creative pursuits, and the woman who can sing or paint or give piano lessons usually feels fulfilled. By far the largest number of American women, however, are entering the labor market. Over one third of all women in this country are now engaged in full-time or part-time employment.

It is little wonder, therefore, that women are seeking equal employment opportunities, and equitable treatment in society as a whole. But it is also clear that the ultimate goal which women seek lies far beyond that of equal pay for equal work or the freedom to apply for credit cards or equal returns on Social Security benefits. What modern American women are really after is the freedom to be whole persons, and this has been explicitly stated by the feminists. In the words of Betty Friedan: "We speak for the right of every woman in America to become all she is capable of becoming—on her own and/or in partnership with a man. . . . Women, above all, want to say what their own lives are going to be, what their own personalities are going to be, not permitting male experts to define what is 'feminine' or isn't or should be." [36] Perhaps one of the best statements of the women's goals was made by Elizabeth Duncan Koontz:

This is also what men seek

. . . let us be clear in our own minds about what we really want. Is it equal pay, equal job opportunities, equal rights? Or are these just victories along the way to some larger goal? I believe there is a larger goal that we pursue. I believe that what women must have is freedom—the freedom to choose different life styles, the freedom to fulfill the best that is in them. A philosopher once said: "The great law of culture is: Let each become all that he was created capable of being." I do not think we ask for more than that. I am convinced we cannot settle for less.[37]

In short, the moderate feminists are not saying that every woman should go out and get a job. They fully recognize that some women find the fullest development of their capabilities in homemaking and should be allowed to do so. What they are saying is that women should have the freedom to choose what they want to do and what they want to be, without being penalized in some way for that choice, whether by low wages or social disapproval or the necessity of choosing between home and career. Those are penalties that are not forced on men, and they should not be forced on women either, by the stereotyped definitions of woman's role and femininity which have been fostered in the past in our society.

If women achieve these goals, it is clear that the total value structure of our society will be altered. There is little doubt that primary worth is now placed upon success, productivity, efficiency, and consumption, and that everything is sacrificed to those ends. Sociologist Alice S. Rossi has drawn a vivid picture of the effect of such current values on the American home:

Behind the veneer of modern emancipation is a woman isolated in an apartment or suburban home, exclusively responsible for the care of young children, dependent on her husband for income . . . and urged to buy more and more clothes and household possessions, which she then takes more time but little pleasure in maintaining. Complementing

the life of the woman in [this] . . . model of sex roles, the
American male is prodded to seek success and achievement
in a competitive job world at the emotional cost of limited
time or psychic energy for his marriage or his children,
tempted by the same consumption-stimulating media and
promises of easy credit, expected to uproot his family if a
move "is good for his career," and ridiculed if he seeks to
participate more extensively in home and child care as
"unmanly." [38]

It must be recognized, moreover, that the value structure which this picture represents forms a formidable
obstacle to the realization of feminist goals. Our producing, consuming society is predicated on the assumption
that women will stay at home and tend the house and
children, and thus free their men to throw their whole
time and effort into maintaining high levels of efficiency
and creativity on the job. If women do not stay at home
and are not content to be merely supportive of their
husbands, but demand the right to pursue activities
outside the home of equal importance with those of their
husbands, then there are some fundamental questions
that will have to be answered: Who will take care of the
children? Will the state? Is that what we want? To quote
Dr. Abram Kardiner again: "You can't pay anyone to love
your child. The monogamous family is the perfect envi-
ronment for child development, for the incubation of
feelings. I think you're dealing with dynamite when you
toy with it." [39]

If men take on increasing responsibility for home and
family, what will happen to their productivity, and to the
gross national product? Can our standard of living
possibly remain so high? If we do not utilize women's
talents and education to the full, are we not wasting a
national resource on a mammoth scale? Was not Harriet
Van Horne correct when she said, "The most serious
brain drain in the world is the drain in the kitchen sink;
down, down go the wit, the dreams, the talent of millions

of women"? Can we as a nation value persons more, and products less, and yet maintain our standard of life? Can we make the adjustments in our values necessary for such a revolution?

The fact is that we are making them. Creaking and groaning and straining at the seams, our society is nevertheless changing its ways, working out new patterns of marriage and work and family responsibility, and apparently placing new value on a nonmaterialistic way of life. To cite one example, polls now show that many of our young people in college are opting for other values besides that of "success" in business. One poll revealed that 88 percent of those college students surveyed indicated that they would prefer a career in government or academic life to a career in business. Another found that all thirty-nine editors of the *Harvard Law Review,* the law school's top and most promising students, preferred careers in poverty affairs, environmental concerns, consumer protection and social reforms, rather than in the industrial world.[40] This lessening of the desire to compete and to succeed in the marketplace was forecast among the activist college youth of the 1960's, who in dress and mores largely spurned traditional materialistic values. Yet such findings must be balanced against the current student stampede to enter medicine, the highest paid profession in the country. Values are very much in transition right now in our society, but what the final outcome will be is anybody's guess. There is no doubt, however, that the women's movement is both a fundamental sign of change as well as one of the principal factors in bringing it about.

We therefore come to our principal questions: Are the goals of the women's movement compatible with Biblical faith? Are the freedom and personhood that the feminists seek, desirable and even possible in Christian marriage?

The answers to both questions would seem an unqualified "Yes," and yet, strangely enough, there are those who would not give that answer. If one studies the history of the church with regard to the position of women, there is no doubt that Simone de Beauvoir was right when she said, "Christian ideology has contributed no little to the oppression of women." There are still those who would use the Christian faith to limit women to their traditional role as housewife and mother. Consider the following letter written to the editor of *The National Observer* from a woman in Bountiful, Utah:

> I believe it to be an unfortunate situation when a woman finds herself frustrated and incomplete in her role as mother and wife. This feeling of monotony and despair need not exist in the mind of a woman if her thinking is beyond self. Self is crucified when people, male like female, have fellowship with Christ. When this religious concept is abandoned then there is an abundance of room within the individual for the growth of a number of maladies . . . ingratitude, irresponsibility, neglect, unloving, temperamental [sic], harshness, and selfishness.
>
> Instead of the woman placing on her life's menu what is best for her child or husband she fills it rather with a trite expression, "I'm bored."
>
> Woman will feel trapped and will be on the prowl as long as she is empty from within. A master's or doctorate cannot bring peace to the mind and soul. She can seek all means to escape her responsibilities as a mother and wife only to discover in later years that she forsook the blessings of womanhood for extra income or prestige.[41]

For this woman, the wife's place is in the home, and the Christian faith is a means of keeping her there, used as a whitewash to cover over all our problems. This solution distorts the nature of the Christian faith and uses it to hide from reality.

More seriously, there are those within the radical feminist movement who maintain that it is impossible for a woman to have the freedom to live as a person in her own right and to be a Christian at the same time. One of the most articulate champions of this view has been Mary

Daly. In her book *Beyond God the Father*[42] and in her "Feminist Postchristian Introduction" to the second edition of her 1968 work, *The Church and the Second Sex*,[43] she has maintained that Christian symbols and doctrines themselves are so oriented toward patriarchal supremacy that it is impossible for a liberated woman to adopt them. "Sexism," she writes, is "inherent in the symbol system of Christianity itself"—for example, God is spoken of as "Father"—and "a primary function of Christianity in Western culture has been to legitimize sexism." [44] Also, like so many radical feminists, Daly sees marriage as a "burial" (p. 29), as "imprisonment" (p. 30), as a "disaster" (p. 35). Therefore, in her view, Christian marriage would probably be the absolutely worst possible fate.

These negative views concerning the Christian faith have had an influence on many women. For example, the Women's Center for Theologizing in Kansas City has made this statement:

> . . . the Christian faith is so bound up in traditional [male] theological language and concepts that it is sometimes impossible to expand concepts when feminist issues are raised. The question then is raised: When a woman says her experience does not fit the Christian understanding of life, should we encourage her to leave the faith? Or to try to see that her feelings really do fit, at some level, the Christian experience? Our answer, as yet incomplete, and different for every woman, lies in suggesting that a variety of ingredients compose the source of authority for our faith, and each one takes precedence at a different time: Scripture, tradition, reason, and our own perceptions.[45]

This latter quotation probably best gets at the real heart of the problem involved: What is the authority on which we base our decisions and views and actions? For the radical feminists, it has become their own perception of reality, "thinking out of experience," to use Daly's words (*The Church and the Second Sex*, p. 49). The authority of God, of Christ, of the Scriptures as they mediate the revelation of God, is denied. In fact, Daly states that women should not try to serve the Biblical God, revealed in Jesus Christ, because "the Second Sex, dreaming of transcendence, would find itself forever supine on the Procrustean bed of 'the Sovereign Lord' " (p. 47).

There is the most incredible naiveté about the sinfulness of human nature manifested in these radical views. They assume that our own perceptions of reality will not be warped by our selfishness and pride, our rationalizations and attempts at self-justification, our ego-defenses and hatreds. It is no accident that the Women's Center for Theologizing says it has great difficulty with the Christian doctrine of sin, not to mention the incarnation.[46] It is also no accident that Daly's most recent works—written since she has left the Catholic faith—are simply shot through with a hatred for everything male, which effectively eliminates the experience of half of the human race from her purview.

I prefer to be realistic, which means for me, radically Christian, since it really is only the Christian faith that makes sense out of life. We are indeed shortsighted and sinful human beings, created to live in a loving relationship with the God who made us through Jesus Christ, and with our fellow human beings. We are given the merciful gift of marriage by that same loving God, and shown through the revelation of that God in Jesus Christ how to live in the Christian relation of matrimony, abundantly and joyfully. It is the Scriptures that mediate to us such revelation, and it is the Scriptures that therefore form the final, dynamic authority for our faith and practice. What, then, does the Bible have to say about the place of woman within marriage? Are its views compatible with full freedom and personhood for men *and* women? It is these questions with which we will deal in the next chapter.

CHAPTER 5

Free and Equal
in Christ

Unless the LORD builds the house,
those who build it labor in vain.
—Ps. 127:1

Does the Bible affirm the full personhood of woman and man, and is that personhood possible within the context of Christian marriage? There is no doubt whatsoever that the answer to both questions is, Yes!

There are two creation stories in the Old Testament. The later one in Gen. 1:1 to 2:4a is from Priestly circles of the sixth century B.C.; the earlier one in Gen. 2:4b–24 is from the tenth century B.C. In the first of these stories, it is stated that both male and female are created in the image of God,[47] and no differentiation is made between their individual possession of the image.[48] Both are something like their Creator, equally akin to him.

Moreover, both male and female are given the image of God in order that they may have dominion over the earth (Gen. 1:26, 28), exercising equal lordship over every nonhuman creature and over the natural world as a whole. Man and woman are glorious creatures, given like sovereignty over the earth. However, that sovereignty is always second to God's, from whom they receive all their endowments, including the power to propagate and the power to rule. They are God's images, and just as in ancient times, an emperor would erect images of himself in distant parts of his realm to show his sovereignty over it, so we are, figuratively, God's little images, put upon earth to show his ultimate lordship over it. Our rule over the world is to point to God's rule. In the words of Jesus, "Let your light so shine before men, that they may see your good works and give glory to your Father who is in heaven" (Matt. 5:16). This finally is the purpose of human life: to glorify the God who made us. We are his stewards of his creation.

A higher and more worthy purpose for human life could not be found, and it is a purpose given to both male and female. Over against all views of human beings that would degrade them to the level of animals, or make them expendable as tools of power or politics, or waste them as fodder for cannons, or enslave them as servants of the state or of ideologies or of history, or define them as puppets of deterministic forces this confession of faith made in Gen. 1:26 ff. says, No, you are gloriously made in the image of God. And over against all views that would elevate persons to the status of gods or centers of absolute power and will the confession says, Give glory to him! It is such human nature that is "very good" (Gen. 1:31), and it is in such purpose for our lives that our highest good and happiness are to be found.

In the second creation story, in Gen. 2:4b–24, male and female are both the careful creations of the Lord. The man is shaped from the dust of the ground, intimately, in the hands of God the potter (Gen. 2:7; cf. Job 10:8–12; Ps. 139:13). The woman is formed from the rib of the man, secretly, by a special act of God, the Father of the bride (Gen. 2:21–22). The language is all poetic and confessional, to be understood as the story of us all: "Adam" in the story is the Hebrew word for "mankind." The author is telling us that this is our story, a picture of our relation to our Creator.[49]

The fact that the woman is created from the rib of the man is most significant for the author of Gen., ch. 2. The man and woman were originally one flesh, and after the creation of the woman they long to become one again. This reunion is realized in the ecstatic oneness of marital love:

> "This at last is bone of my bones
> and flesh of my flesh. . . ."

Therefore a man leaves his father and his mother and cleaves to his wife, and they become one flesh. (Gen. 2:23–24.)

The author is making the confession of faith that marriage, the body, sexual desire and union, the resulting home and children, are all gifts of a loving Creator and have nothing evil about them. For this reason, the Old Testament celebrates sex (cf. the Song of Songs; Prov. 30:19), the wife "like a fruitful vine," children "like olive shoots around your table" (Ps. 128:3; cf. Ps. 144:12), the sons of one's youth: "Happy is the man who has his quiver full of them!" (Ps. 127:5). There is celebration of life here, in all its fructescence and earthy goodness, an actual reveling and glee in the goodness of the physical. It is as if this author too is joining in that hymnic salute of Gen. 1:31: "And God saw everything that he had made, and behold, it was very good."

There is no hint here whatever of any superior or inferior station. As we pointed out in Chapter 1, the wife who is created from the rib, is the one who "corresponds" to the man, who reflects back to him the nature of his being ("This at last is bone of my bones and flesh of my flesh") and thus can be loved as himself ("He who loves his wife loves himself," Eph. 5:28; "You shall love your neighbor as yourself," Lev. 19:18; Mark 12:31 and pars.). There is here only a joy and relief that oneness and companionship have at last been found, and the confession that such wondrous gifts have been given by a very good God. Such is the nature of the marital union as the Lord meant it to be.

Genesis does not, however, indulge in romantic idealism. It knows also that there is a dreadful disruption which has turned sour our joy, marred our marriages, and set male against female. It knows also that many of us have corrupted God's good gift of marital oneness, so that we now view marriage from only the cynic's disillusionment with it or the lover's grief over its failure.

So Genesis also tells a story about the brokenness of our relationships. In the ancient story of Adam and Eve in the garden, in Gen., ch. 3, the primal couple—who are really symbols for us all—eat of the forbidden fruit. Their motive is to become their own gods, and to make the real God unnecessary. "You will be like God," the serpent says to Eve (Gen. 3:5). In other words, Adam and Eve no longer want to understand themselves in relation to their Creator. They want to understand themselves and their life solely on their own terms. They want to shape their lives according to their own humanistic desires. They want to be captains of their own fate and controllers of their own destiny, planning their own future and setting their own goals.

The result of this attempt to reject God's rule is the disruption of their relationship. Suddenly they no longer know a joyful unity and companionship. Suddenly they become self-conscious "I's" over against each other, disturbed by the fact that they are different and somehow guilty and vulnerable. In the words of Genesis, "Then the eyes of both were opened, and they knew that they were naked; and they sewed fig leaves together and made themselves aprons" (Gen. 3:7). Here, in the most penetrating simplicity, are pictured our glory and our misery: our proud attempts to rule our own lives, and our guilt and our shame about ourselves. In self-defense and justification, we therefore refuse responsibility for self and one another. When God addresses the man and asks him what it is he has done, the man replies by attempting to put the blame elsewhere: "The woman whom thou gavest to be with me, she gave me fruit of the tree, and I ate" (Gen. 3:12). And so too the woman: "The serpent beguiled me, and I ate" (Gen. 3:13). How estranged that once joyful couple has become from each other in their fear and stolen trespass!

The major characteristic of our creaturely existence is, however, that we are responsible to the Lord who made us. So the woman and the man, and always we, bear the consequences of actions taken. In the subsequent judgment, Adam has the joyful gift of his work (cf. Gen. 2:15) turned into toil and drudgery (Gen. 3:17–19), while to the woman, the Lord says:

> I will greatly multiply your pain
>   in childbearing;
>   in pain you shall bring forth children,
>   yet your desire shall be for your husband,
>   and he shall rule over you.
>
> (Gen. 3:16.)

This woman was created to join flesh with her husband in the joyful unity of marital love. Now the childbirth that results from that union becomes a source of pain to the woman and that which threatens her life. Gone is the joy; she knows only now a humiliating domination: ". . . your desire shall be for your husband, and he shall rule over you." The woman still desires her man, she still is lonely, the sexual drive still hungers; but the judgment is that in their union he will be her master.

Here, in profoundest terms, is where the battle of the sexes begins: in our flight from God and our prideful attempts to be our own masters. The rule of man over woman is finally the result of sin, and the intended wholesomeness of the relation between male and female is corrupted because we deny our relationship with God.

Just how the author of Gen., ch. 3, could have laid hold of such a view in the ancient Near Eastern world in the tenth century B.C. seems beyond rational explanation. He must have been grasped by the most radical revelation of God's desire for his universe. Such a view flew in the face of the customs and beliefs of every civilization of the ancient world, and still today it represents a totally unique position. It is nevertheless a proclamation that puts our life as men and women in the proper perspective. The good gift of marriage that God has given us is corrupted and spoiled by us because we are trying to live our lives apart from our Lord and Creator. That is the preface which Genesis sets to all the rest of the Biblical story, and it is in that context that what the rest of the Scriptures have to say about the relation between male and female must be understood.

In the Old Testament, the brokenness of life apart from God is clearly pictured. Woman's role in the remaining stories is always one of subordination to father or husband. That is the way Israel constructed her society in her sin, say the authors. And that is the way we construct our society in our sin too.

Bigamy enters this sinful picture already in Gen. 4:19. Israel's laws always favor the authority of the male. It was the husband only who had the power of divorce (Deut. 24:1–4). Daughters were always considered less desirable than sons (cf. Lev. 12:1–5), and women were always given a lesser value than men (Lev. 27:1–7). A father sometimes had the right to make his daughter a prostitute (Judg. 19:24, but see Lev. 19:29). He could sell her into slavery in payment of his debts (Ex. 21:7; Neh. 5:5). Such enslavement was not lifted at the end of six years, as it was with males (Ex. 21:2–11), and a slave woman could be subjected to very harsh treatment (Gen. 16:1–6).

To be sure, there was some dignity given to the role of women in marriage, in Old Testament times. They lived always within the context of patriarchal authority, and yet within that context they had a degree of freedom and responsibility as wives and mothers. Marriage was never considered merely a transfer of chattel property. There is no example in the Bible where the wife was simply purchased. Sometimes the woman's wishes in the marriage contract were honored (Num. 36:6), and there are many examples in the Old Testament of marriage based on love (Gen. 24:67; 29:20; I Sam. 1:8; Prov. 5:18–19; Song of Songs). Malachi sets forth the personal meaning of marriage by describing the wife as "your companion and your wife by covenant" (Mal. 2:14). This personal relationship was guarded by the stipulation of the death penalty for both an adulterer and an adulteress (Lev. 20:10). The Decalogue demanded equal honor and obedience for both mother and father (Ex. 20:12; Deut. 5:16).

Within Israelite society, women had many functions. They were always present at weddings and funerals, and were the mourners for the dead (cf. II Sam. 1:24). They shared in the work of the harvest, such as the barley harvest (Ruth 2:8), and they were allowed and even praised in economic life (Prov. 31:16 ff., 24). A few of them had enormous influence in affairs of state (Deborah, Judg., ch. 5; Bathsheba, II Sam., chs. 11 ff.; Jezebel, I Kings, chs. 19 ff.). Some were famous as prophetesses (Miriam, Ex. 15:20; Deborah; Huldah, II Kings 22:14), or had official roles in the cult (Neh. 7:67).

Every woman was married in Israel—we hear only of widows, never of spinsters. Although a wife was subject to the authority of her husband, expected to bear his children, to care for them and her home and husband, nevertheless she enjoyed some rights and a measure of freedom and respect within the structure of Hebrew patriarchal society.

The remarkable fact is that over against the laws and

customs of the entire ancient Near East, the author of Gen., ch. 3, could look beyond the structure of his own society to that transcendent ideal of woman's equality with man. He could make the confession of faith that the subordination of woman was not intended by God at all, but was the result of our own sin. When this transcendent vision was lost sight of in postexilic and intertestamental times, and when the law was elevated to a place of supreme importance, sometimes even above God, women were increasingly segregated in Jewish society. They lost what leadership they had in the community. They were segregated in the cult, they were expected to cover their heads in public, and they were not to be addressed on the street. Thus does humanity deal with females when it loses its God, by whom alone the honor and worth of every person are created and preserved.

The actions and words of Jesus therefore intrude once more with alien hope into segregated first-century Jewish society. He freely and naturally engages women in forbidden conversation in public (John 4:7 ff.). His closest friends include Mary and Martha and Mary Magdalene, and everywhere his ministry extends his healing and teaching to females (Matt. 9:20–22; Mark 6:30–44 and pars.; 7:24–30 and par.; 1:29–31 and par.; Luke 13:10–17). Sometimes it is women who are the subject of his parables (Luke 15:8 f.) or sayings (Matt. 24:41 and par.), or who become the models of faith for his disciples (Matt. 15:21–28; Mark 14:3–9 and par.; 12:41–44 and par.). We are told that a number of women accompanied Jesus and his disciples as he went through cities and villages preaching (Luke 8:1–3), providing for the preaching mission out of their own means. According to three of the Gospels, it is women who are the first witnesses and evangelists of the resurrection (Matt. 28:8; Luke 24:9 f.; John 20:18).

Women continue to be of importance in the life of the

New Testament church. In Acts, both males and females are imprisoned by Saul for their Christian belief (Acts 8:3; 9:2). In Acts 18:26, both Aquila and his wife, Priscilla, instruct Apollos in the faith. In II Tim. 1:5, Timothy's mother, Eunice, and his grandmother, Lois, are held up to him as examples of believers. Romans 16:1 reveals that Phoebe and others served as deaconesses in the church, and Heb., ch. 11, does not fail to include Sarah and even Rahab the harlot, from the Old Testament, among the "cloud of witnesses" (Heb. 11:11, 31; 12:1).

The reason for this inclusion of women in the community of believers is not hard to find. They are reinstated there by the life and death and resurrection of Jesus Christ. Whatever else the New Testament has to say about women, it knows beyond all shadow of a doubt that God's Son lived and died and was raised for *all*. Through the sacrifice of his broken body, all have been reconciled again to God, brought back into a living fellowship with the Lord whom we all rejected.

But if we have been reconciled to God, if the separation from him caused by our sin has been bridged by Christ's offered blood and body, then our alienation from one another has also been overcome. Male and female once again have that joyful possibility of living in oneness together. It is exactly that glad possibility to which Paul witnesses:

> For as many of you as were baptized into Christ have put on Christ. There is neither Jew nor Greek, there is neither slave nor free, there is neither male nor female; for you are all one in Christ Jesus. (Gal. 3:27–28; cf. I Cor. 12:13; Col. 3:11.)

The ancient enmity between man and woman, spawned by our rebellion against God, has been quieted and done away by the One born at Bethlehem:

> He is our peace, who has made us both one, and has broken down the dividing wall of hostility. (Eph. 2:14.)

full freedom and equality possible only for Christians.

> By one Spirit we were all baptized into one body. (I Cor. 12:13.)

> In him all the fulness of God was pleased to dwell, and through him to reconcile to himself all things, whether on earth or in heaven, making peace by the blood of his cross. (Col. 1:19–20.)

> You, who once were estranged and hostile in mind . . . he has now reconciled in his body of flesh by his death. (Col. 1:21–22.)

Everywhere the New Testament sings the song of relationships restored, of divided persons reunited with one another, of hostilities overcome and healed. That is the good news of the gospel for every one of our marriages. Woman is restored to her full equality with man. There is in Christ no differentiation in worth or status between male and female. Every hostility that haunts our homes has the possibility of being dissipated by the victory over evil and the power given us in the work of Jesus Christ.

Full freedom and equality and personhood within marriage are therefore not only possible in Christian wedlock, but it is the Christian gospel alone that makes them possible. It is that gospel—the actions of God in Jesus Christ—which alone deals effectively with our sin.

Heaven knows we cannot heal ourselves! Surely the smoldering hatred for men, the haughty self-justifications, the sexual aberrations of the radical feminists, are clear evidence of that fact. When we set out to create our own heaven on earth, we usually wind up with hell. We are feeble gods, you and I, who really are not cut out for the role. Despite our humanitarian impulses and our grand designs for peace and "sisterhood," we spoil it all with our slavery to evil. As Paul put it so long ago:

> I do not understand my own actions. For I do not do what I want, but I do the very thing I hate. . . . I can will what is right, but I cannot do it. For I do not do the good I want, but

the evil I do not want is what I do. . . . Wretched man that I am! Who will deliver me from this body of death? (Rom. 7:15, 18–19, 24.)

The women's movement has dreamed a marvelous dream; it has willed "what is right" in many instances. But of itself, apart from the work of Christ, it cannot realize that dream. In this sense, "women's liberation" is an ironic misnomer for the movement, for it assumes that somehow we have the power within us to liberate ourselves from the effects of our sin, to create our own "balm in Gilead to heal the sin-sick soul." As Jeremiah knew, who created the figure, only God has the proper balm, and apart from him "the health of the daughter of my people" will not be restored (Jer. 8:22).

It is high time that the church, we Christians, realize these facts, and alter our approach to the feminist movement in this country. We have for years confessed that salvation, abundant life, release from slavery to sin, reconciliation with God and one another come only through the work of Jesus Christ in our midst. Yet, when we have been confronted with the feminist movement, we have forgotten that confession of faith. We have assumed that somehow—through consciousness raising or through altering our language or through setting up task forces on women's rights—we will in fact *create* freedom and equality for women. The truth is that freedom and equality for all persons have already been created through the cross and resurrection.

. . . if the Son makes you free, you will be free indeed. (John 8:36.)

You were bought with a price; do not become slaves of men. (I Cor. 7:23.)

For freedom Christ has set us free; stand fast therefore, and do not submit again to a yoke of slavery. (Gal. 5:1.)

It is the church's responsibility, therefore, and the individual Christian's responsibility to lay hold of that freedom and equality within our own life, to live it out in every sphere, and to proclaim it and to witness to it, uncompromisingly, to the world. The proclamation and life of freedom is part of our Christian witness to the world. If we do not so testify in word and deed, we are not proclaiming the gospel which was delivered to us to take into all the world, and we are therefore leaving men and women enslaved within the bondage of their evil. "Who will deliver . . . [us] from this body of death?" (Rom. 7:24)—Christ already has! And that is very good news for every one of our homes.

Let the church therefore first put its own house in order. Paradoxically, no institution in our society has been more reluctant to grant equal rights to women than has the body of Christ itself. We deny our gospel before the cynical eyes of the world when we deny freedom of status and function to any person, male or female. We need not rehearse here the sorry record of the church's stance toward its women members. Feminist books are full of the sad details of discrimination, in the ministry, in leadership positions, in wages paid and opportunities denied. We have too often proclaimed a gospel that we have not lived, as not only the women but also the blacks, the poor, the social outcasts can readily attest. "Personhood" has been a word on our lips, but often far from our hearts (cf. Isa. 29:13), and though most of the major denominations are now trying to correct the situation, we have a long, long way yet to go.

Failing to stand fast in its freedom, the church has continually submitted to new yokes of slavery. That has always been a temptation for the church. If it were not so, Paul would not have had to deliver that admonition to the congregation in Galatia, in Gal. 5:1, which we have quoted. Indeed, over against the proclamation of full personhood in Christ, the New Testament itself contains several attempts to subject freed Christian women to the traditional yoke of patriarchal society. The passages, all of which are found in letters written to Christian congregations in the first and beginning of the second century A.D., are well known and well despised by the feminists. Perhaps it will be helpful if we comment briefly on them.

There is first of all Paul's regulation for worship in the Corinthian church, found in I Cor. 14:33b–35:

> As in all the churches of the saints, the women should keep silence in the churches. For they are not permitted to speak, but should be subordinate, as even the law says. If there is anything they desire to know, let them ask their husbands at home. For it is shameful for a woman to speak in church.

This is a strange regulation coming from one who has repeatedly fought against slavery to the law in the conviction that we are no longer under law but under grace (cf. Romans and Galatians). The fact is that Paul himself contradicts the regulation. In I Cor. 11:4–16, he allows women to prophesy in church just as long as they have their society's customary decency to cover their heads.

The contradiction points up the situation in which Paul found himself with the Corinthians. They apparently were a particularly contentious congregation, engaging in sexual immorality (I Cor. 5:1; 6:16 ff.), hauling one another into court (I Cor. 6:1), slandering the apostle himself (I Cor. 4:3 ff.), engaging in worship of idols (I Cor. 10:14 ff.), dividing into factious divisions (I Cor. 1:10 ff.; 11:17 ff.), and even getting drunk at the Lord's Supper (I Cor. 11:21). Even their worship services sometimes turned into utter bedlam as they vied with one another to speak in tongues (I Cor. 14:1 ff.). It did not help matters any that there was in the group an especially cantankerous and squawking bunch of women, who took advantage of their newfound freedom to sound forth whenever they felt like it. Paul deals with all these problems in turn, and he also deals with the squawking women: "Shut up!" he tells them in effect, "Let us have a little order!" just as he tells the men sometimes to remain silent also (I Cor. 14:29–30). Paul's concern is thoroughly practical; he is striving for some decency and quiet in worship, and he tries to shame the women into silence. His means are not consistent with his own proclaimed gospel, but when one reads of Paul's struggles with the Corinthians, the restrictions certainly are understandable.

I Timothy and Titus are even more traditional in their view of women's role:

> . . . women should adorn themselves modestly and sensibly in seemly apparel, not with braided hair or gold or pearls or costly attire but by good deeds, as befits women who profess religion. Let a woman learn in silence with all submissiveness. I permit no woman to teach or to have authority over men; she is to keep silent. For Adam was formed first, then Eve; and Adam was not deceived, but the woman was deceived and became a transgressor. Yet woman will be saved through bearing children, if she continues in faith and love and holiness, with modesty. (I Tim. 2:9–15.)
>
> Bid the older women likewise to be reverent in behavior, not to be slanderers or slaves to drink; they are to teach what is good, and so train the young women to love their husbands and children, to be sensible, chaste, domestic, kind, and submissive to their husbands, that the word of God may not be discredited. (Titus 2:3–5.)

Behind the passage in Timothy again lie specific problems in congregations. In this case we do not know where those congregations were, perhaps in Asia Minor. But we know from I Tim. 4:3 that there was a good deal of ferment in marital relations, perhaps as a result of the new Christian freedom for women. Timothy is careful to instruct women members of the congregations not to inflame the desires of men by daring, unseemly dress, but to act with propriety as befits new creatures in Christ. We also learn from II Tim. 3:6–7 that false teachers of religion were gaining access to the women in their homes, leading them astray with false doctrine and perhaps licentious behavior. In I Tim. 5:13, we read that some of the younger widows were "idlers, gadding about from house to house, and not only idlers but gossips and busybodies, saying what they should not." To counteract this activity, women were forbidden to exercise teaching authority in the church and were instructed to pursue their traditional role. If they did so in faith and love and holiness, they would be saved—not because they bore children, as some mistakenly interpret I Tim. 2:15—but because they had faith in Christ.

In the passage from Titus, the concerns are much the same, although there we read that the error of the women was slandering and drunkenness. The women are urged to their traditional sensible and domestic role in order "that the word of God may not be discredited." The new Christians, it seems, had used their freedom as an opportunity to commit other evils, bringing condemnation on themselves and on the faith they professed. The remedy urged upon them therefore is a return to behavior at least as seemly as that of the pagan women—a cure not at all in accord with the gospel, but again certainly comprehensible under the circumstances, and apparently the only one to which the women involved would listen. Timothy and Titus speak with the voice of a church trying to consolidate its position in the Roman world. The shocking behavior of the liberated women added nothing to that cause (cf. I Peter 3:1–6; Col. 3:18), just as it may be said that some radical feminists' foulmouthed, frequent use of four-letter words or defiant advocacy of homosexuality adds nothing to the cause of women's rights today. As Paul puts it, "You were called to freedom; . . . do not use your freedom as an opportunity for the flesh" (Gal. 5:13). Apparently if we do not know how to walk by the Spirit, then we are subjected again to the law.

In all these New Testament passages, as is also the case in I Peter 3:1–6 and Col. 3:18, we are dealing not only with situations in specific congregations but also with writers who have by no means abandoned all their traditional views of women's place. We sometimes think that the New Testament church was perfect. It was not. Its members, leaders, teachers, and writers had fully as much difficulty in living out the gospel as we do today. (Just think of the disputes that arose between Peter and Paul, Gal. 2:11 ff.!) That some of the New Testament writers may have been "male chauvinists" no more invalidates the freedom and personhood given to all persons in Christ Jesus than does the refusal of the Roman Catholic Church today to ordain women to its priesthood. We stumble over these New Testament passages because they are contained in our canon, but so are many passages admonishing slaves to be submissive to their masters (Col. 3:22; Eph. 6:5 ff.; I Tim. 6:1 f.; Titus 2:9; I Peter 2:18 ff.). On the latter subject, however, the light of the gospel has shown in our hearts a little more brightly than is often the case with respect to woman's role. The church has always had trouble living up to its gospel, and the New Testament gives evidence that such has been true from the time of the church's founding. We can only be grateful that we are saved by grace and not by our works!

To make the record complete, we should look at one final passage, in Eph. 5:21–33, on which I base so much of the thought in this book about the relationship of marriage. Again this passage is set in the traditional context of the ancient Near East, where the husband was expected to be head of his household, an expectation that is still also typical in much of American society. In the light

Eph. 5

of the Christian faith, some earthshaking qualifications are introduced into that expectation, and actually the passage is addressed more to husbands than it is to wives. A commandment to both, however, opens the pericope:

> Be subject to one another out of reverence for Christ. (Eph. 5:21.)

That is the theme of the passage: husband and wife are both mutually to be subject to one another, because as they act toward one another, they are acting toward Christ. It is the same thought as our Lord stated in Matt. 25:40: "Truly, I say to you, as you did it to one of the least of these my brethren, you did it to me." Our actions toward our spouses are counted as actions toward the Son of God.

Each side of this mutual subjection is then discussed. Wives are to be subject to their husbands as the church is subject to the Lord (Eph. 5:22–24). Certainly this does not mean that wives are to worship their husbands, to obey them unquestioningly, or to elevate them to the place of God. The New Testament and the Old Testament writers would recoil in horror before such an idolatrous suggestion (cf. Ex. 20:3)! Rather, wives are to act toward their husbands as the church should act toward Christ— in faithfulness, in love, in service, in honor, in devotion— because what the wife does to her husband, she is in fact doing to Christ. If she is unfaithful, nagging, complacent, or hostile toward him, she so treats her Lord.

The writer then turns to husbands, and the rest of the passage deals with them. They are to love their wives "as Christ loved the church and gave himself up for her" (Eph. 5:25), not because they are absolute lords over their wives, but because the church is the body of Christ (Eph. 5:30). Once again, what they do to their wives is what they are doing to Christ (Eph. 5:28–30). Christ loves his body, the church, and so "he who loves his wife loves himself" (Eph. 5:28). The thought is somewhat difficult, but internally consistent, and fully in line with the second great commandment, "You shall love your neighbor as yourself." Husbands are to love their wives and give themselves up for them, as Christ loved his church and gave himself up for her—with the same faithfulness and forgiveness,[50] commitment and caring. Obviously there can be no thought here of the husband's tyranny over his wife or of her humiliating subjection to his domination. In the ancient Near Eastern world this was the revolutionary impact of the passage. Instead, husbands are to serve their wives as Christ served his church, pouring themselves out for their spouses in a sacrificial devotion akin to Christ's. If they are unfaithful or domineering or uncaring or hostile toward their wives, that is the way they are treating the body of Christ; they are doing it to the Lord.

Ephesians 5:31–33 then sum up the thought. Marriage is the symbol of Christ's relation with his church, and each partner in marriage is therefore to act toward the other as he would toward the Lord.

The passage is ingenious. It has preserved the traditional view of the male as the head of the family, but that headship is a function only, not a matter of status or superiority. The understanding of the headship and of the wife's relation to it has been radically transformed. There is no lording it over the other here, no exercise of sinful power, no room for unconcern or hostility toward the other. Instead there is only the full devotion of love, poured out for the other, in imitation of Christ's faithfulness and yearning and sacrifice for his church, and of the church's like response to him. In short, there is here that total and loving commitment which we discussed in Chapter 3. Contrary to the views of many of the feminists, we should have no difficulty in saying yes to this passage as the most perfect pattern for Christian mar-

riage. Who can improve on the love of Christ for us? If
husbands and wives were to love one another as Christ
has loved us his people, and as his people are therefore to
love him in return, there would be no need for this book or
any other on the subject of marriage.

Can we doubt, moreover, that in Jesus Christ we see
humanity at its finest, the picture truly of what it means
to be fully human? In his book *On Becoming a Person,*
psychoanalyst Carl Rogers maintains that the most important factor in developing selfhood is the strength to be
a unique person, responsible for oneself, living "in a way
which is deeply satisfying to me, and which truly expresses me." [51] He tries to enable persons to drop their
facades of personality, to choose their own goals apart
from "oughts" and others' expectations, to become responsible for themselves, to trust themselves, to be open
to new experiences, and to accept others and reality. In
short, Rogers aims for genuineness in the human personality, for expression of the self that one truly is, for
responsibility, for acceptance of reality. In this light,
there was no more genuine person than Jesus of Naza-
reth. He had no phoniness about him, no ducking of
responsibility for his actions, no attempt to be something
other than he was, no avoidance of others' faults, no
shying away from the hard nature of reality. To all this
the cross is eloquent testimony.

But there was another element in the mix of the
personality of the Master, an element that Rogers has
overlooked. While being totally himself, Jesus was totally
faithful to God. His will and God's will were one, a union
born out of his determination to trust God in all circumstances, even unto death. It was his trust in his Father
that made him the most genuine representative of the
human personality as it was meant to be.

We are created to love and serve God. We can be
genuine human beings, fully expressing our real nature,

only when we know ourselves responsible to God alone and take on that responsibility in the form of trusting, caring service to him and to those with whose lives he has entrusted us. We become genuine human beings finally only by faith, out of love for the God who has loved us. This is what it means to be a person: to trust as Jesus trusted, to serve as he served. In the words of Eph. 5:1 once again, to "be imitators of God," to "walk in love, as Christ loved us and gave himself up for us." Or, in Eph. 4:13, to grow up "to mature manhood, to the measure of the stature of the fulness of Christ," to live and act and believe as he did among us.

Contrary to popular misunderstanding, such genuine personhood is not a submersion of self, not a "living through another," not an absorption of one human being into another or a subjection of one person to another who is stronger. It is not a suppression or distortion of one's own personality, but the fullest possible exercise of one's own genuine personality. Rogers has maintained that if a husband or wife says to the other, "I commit myself wholly to you and your welfare," or "I am more concerned for you than I am for myself," this seemingly "beautiful attitude" can lead to a submergence of self which is fatal to the partnership.[52] Of course it can, if God is left out of the picture!

God calls us not to the loss of our personalities, but to the full exercise of them: "You shall love the Lord your God with *all* your heart, and with *all* your soul, and with *all* your mind, and with *all* your strength" (Mark 12:30 and pars., italics added). I am called to affirm all my talents and characteristics—the desires and cares of my heart, the transcendent visions of my soul, the abilities of my intellect, the workings and wants of my body. They are gifts God has given me, and I am to affirm them as real and valuable, and to praise him for the person he has made me. But then I am to use all these gifts in the service of his will and purpose. In that service, he holds me responsible for loving and serving my fellow human beings. "You shall love your neighbor as yourself." Above all, he holds me responsible for loving and serving my mate, whose life, by his gracious will, has been joined intimately with mine. The Christian faith holds the human personality sacred because God made us. It also holds us totally responsible for trusting and serving that Creator by serving our fellows. Out of those two continuing affirmations—of self as created by God, and of responsibility to God's will—can grow the development of genuine personhood akin to that of Christ's. The Christian faith is not only compatible with the full exercise of personhood; it alone makes it possible.

Now how do we apply all of this within the actual relationships of our marriages? First of all, we must always take care that our lives are structured in such a way that both partners in the marriage can in fact fully exercise all their hearts and souls and minds and strength. With respect to husbands, our competitive, consuming, success-oriented culture has so programmed males' lives that the emotional and relational portions of their personalities—their hearts and souls—have been emasculated. They are not expected to value warmth and intimacy, friendship and love. They are expected to compete, to tackle jobs, to overcome obstacles, to seize the offensive, to turn out the product. They are steam-pressured into conformity to company policy and mores, into neglect of their homes and families to gain promotion, into expenditure of all energy and creativity behind a desk or jetting from conference to consultation. Nothing is more important in society's eyes than the latest company profits and performance on the job. The one who can best perform and compete is the one who wins.

The result is that this depersonalized male machine runs into trouble in his middle years. Those who have not performed and won, feel themselves to be failures; those who have, often find their achievements empty reward for their effort. Suddenly they realize that they are existing without a purpose for it all, without anyone or anything with whom they can be fully human. Some turn back to their homes and try to become fathers and husbands again, but all too often they find their families have become to them as strangers and have learned to live without their presence interrupting the daily routine. Others turn to extramarital affairs, looking for the intimacy and warmth they have long neglected. Some divorce and remarry in an effort to begin all over again; perhaps "the second time around," they think, they can include love in their lives. Unfortunately, however, one does not learn overnight how to be a person with a heart and a soul. As Ellen Goodman has put it, "They often find it enormously difficult to learn the language and habits of feelings." [53]

In short, the role that our society has assigned to many of its male white-collar workers is a role that has prevented many husbands from exercising their hearts and souls as full persons, in the relationship of their marriage. Those who have successfully resisted such emasculation of their personalities and marriages have been those who have realized that the pursuit of the dollar, and of social status based on economic worth, is not the ultimate goal in life. Man has not been created to serve mammon but God—and love and fellowship with one's family is a blessed form of that latter service.

It has been the contention of many in the feminist movement that the liberation of women from their sole roles as supporters for the husbands' economic "success" will free men also from the confining pressures of their occupations. Women will share fully in supporting the family economically, men will take over more of the home-keeping and child-rearing responsibilities. For example, Alice Rossi maintains that our society must be completely restructured to the point where family, community, and play are considered to be as important as politics and work for all. A man's time spent with his family, she argues, must be considered as important as his time spent on the job. A woman's time spent in creativity outside her home must be valued as highly as her hours spent with her children.[54]

It is a noble vision; the women's movement has had lots of noble visions. The feminists base their hope for such a possibility on the fact that modern Sweden, since 1968, by means of education, has deliberately created a society where men and women share fully in economic life and homemaking. To make such a society possible, the state has taken over wide-ranging responsibility for home functions. Couples receive basic child allowance; there are child-care centers, free maternity care, maternity benefit payments, allowances to families with handicapped children, free school meals, municipal domestic help for emergencies, subsidized holiday camps for children.[55] Whether or not it is desirable to turn the care of children over to the state is a real question, however, and we have to ask if the effects on the family unit and on the economic life of the nation are in the long run beneficial.

There are a few marriages in the United States in which husband and wife have successfully switched traditional roles, with the wife working and the husband tending the home. And there are now millions of marriages in which both parents are employed, though the spouses' functions remain largely traditional in such homes, with the wife expected not only to hold down a job but also to care for the home as well. Consider the following complaint, written to the syndicated Dorothy Dix newspaper column:

> Ever since I went back to work seven months ago my husband has been after me to give him my pay check. When I refuse he sulks.
>
> After all, I hold down two jobs: one at home, the other at

the office. I get no pay, much less thanks, for the former and it involves more work: up at six every morning, dress baby and myself, tidy the house, start breakfast and organize the day's schedule for our baby sitter (an elderly neighbor) who comes at 8:30 and stays till I return at 5:30. By night I'm worn out but there is still dinner to prepare and baby to put to bed.

Weekends instead of taking a holiday, I clean house, catch up with mending and care for our baby. I pay my own medical expenses: oculist, and dentist bills, buy baby's clothes and mine and, if there's a cent left, bank it in a savings account.

Last evening my husband came across with a new attack on my poor little overworked salary; use it to pay half the living expenses! Am I wrong in refusing my husband's request? Should I hand over half my salary to him after deducting the baby sitter's pay?—Harassed Wife.[56]

Obviously there is no "liberation" involved in this marriage, on the part of either husband or wife!

It is doubtful, in fact, that any secular view of liberation can adequately free either male or female from his or her traditional marital roles in our society. It takes a new vision of society, to be sure, but a vision that rises out of a conviction about our ultimate responsibility to God for the full exercise of our personalities, a conviction that knows that "man does not live by bread alone." What God we worship and serve makes all the difference when it comes to setting our goals in life. The man who knows that he is finally responsible to God alone is much less likely to be steam-pressured into a drive for economic success than is the man who sets only human goals, even if they be worthwhile ones such as family happiness and sharing. Our human goals have a way of crumbling before society's pressures. A living relationship with God through Jesus Christ can stand up to almost anything.

Similarly, the woman who knows that her husband must first of all exercise his full heart and soul, as well as his mind and strength, in relationship to God is much less likely to badger that man for material possessions and status to adorn her house and her own role in society. She desires first of all that her husband be fully human. We have defined that humanness in the context of the Christian faith—a loving, trusting, caring, faithful, whole person in relation to God and his family and neighbors. Thus she does not lay upon him the demands of a secular and materialistic society. She lives in Christian liberty in relation to her husband.

In the same manner, husbands foster Christian liberty when they allow their wives to exercise their full personhood, including their minds and strengths, within the relationship of marriage. Many husbands would maintain that they have allowed their wives to be whole persons, and yet they have hidden from themselves an important truth. They really want to be better than their wives, because they never want their wives to challenge their superiority by outperforming them. If the wife should earn more money or recognition on her job than does the husband, such husbands feel somehow shamed, just as they feel equally shamed if their wives can beat them at tennis or golf.

Unfortunately in our culture, the worth of an individual is judged by what he or she achieves. Whether a man is playing tennis or working at his job, his value is judged on the basis of how well he performs. To succeed in America is not primarily "to be," but rather always "to do," "to accomplish," "to achieve." It is the male primarily who is expected to achieve, while the female has always been the one who was expected to support and to "live through" his achievement. She was to stay at home and run his household, raise his children, and give him comfort and security and happiness, so that each day he could face the competitive fray anew. The man in our society is the one who does; the woman is to help him do. Thus, in a very subtle way in our culture, the man is the one who has worth.

All unknowingly, Christian husbands have accepted such valuation of male and female. Therefore they feel threatened and jealous if their wives manage also to achieve, especially if the wife's achievement seems greater than their own. Women for years have known that fact. By the time they reach adolescence, most females have had drummed into them the lesson which the heroine learned in *Annie Get Your Gun*—that you "can't get a man" by outperforming him, whether with a gun or anything else. The result has been that many talented young women have sat on their talents. The beautiful, intelligent girl has decided to be beautiful but dumb. The accomplished sportswoman has begun to flub a few shots. The class valedictorian in high school has often settled for B's in college. The girl who wanted a Ph.D. has given it up for an engagement ring, often putting her hubby through graduate school by pounding a typewriter instead. The sad fact is that husbands have readily accepted such sacrifices and have considered them to be normal.

Christian husbands should know better and certainly should do better if they in fact affirm the full implications and freedom given to females in the Christian faith. Indeed, it is Christian husbands who should uncompromisingly refuse to allow their wives to exercise anything less than the full talents of heart, soul, mind, and strength which God has given them. Wives should be encouraged by their husbands to educate and use their minds and to perform to the full extent of their abilities. Husbands should see to it that roles in the home are adjusted in such a way that full growth and exercise of personality are made possible for their mates. Otherwise husbands are not living out the Christian gospel, and they are not following the second great commandment by loving their wives as they love themselves.

To be sure, there is no set pattern to which each

household should conform. Every couple will have to work out their living arrangements and manner of cooperation on their own. Some wives may work, others may stay at home; some couples will share all functions equally, others will remain in the traditional pattern. Whatever the arrangement, Christian husbands should be as zealous for full freedom for their wives as many of them now still tend to be for their superiority in all things.

To say that this will require new learning and humility on the part of Christian husbands is putting it mildly. True equality for women in the home really contradicts most of our society's expectations. The man who defies those expectations, out of faith, may be laughed at as "unmanly," as lacking in male authority and proper machismo; he may be unjustly labeled henpecked or be pitied by his colleagues. Above all, he will have to deal with his own deeply ingrained feelings of pride, insecurity, and fear, as his wife learns to achieve on his level. It is threatening to live intimately with one as accomplished and smart as you are. It takes a great measure of maturity and self-confidence to allow another to share your level of accomplishment, prestige, and respect. But the husband who gets over his own insecurity and fear is also being liberated from evil, and he is affording his wife the opportunity to use all the talents God has given her. He is, in truth, living out the implications of the gospel of freedom.

When a husband and wife learn, in trust, to afford each other such Christian freedom, they make possible for themselves a life far deeper than any they have previously known. The husband, over against the competitive pressures of our society, is given that love and intimacy which he so desperately needs in our depersonalized world. The wife, secure in the relationship of love with her husband, is lent a firm base of support for her exercise of her independent talents in the community. We all need that one-to-one, deeply intimate and personal relationship, which affords us both security and the independence to be ourselves. There is no partnership that can more satisfyingly provide that firm base than the love and support of a truly Christian marriage.

Paul's admonition not to use our Christian freedom as an opportunity for evil (Gal. 5:13) is again applicable here, especially applicable to the actions of some women.

The feminists, including some who are Christian, have made the mistake in the current struggle for women's rights, of absolutizing their own freedom. They have forgotten that they are called by God to live in relationships, and instead have become centers of absolute will. Nowhere is this more evident than in the complex debate over abortion. Those women who favor abortion on demand claim the right to have sole authority over their own bodies, to have the freedom to say completely on their own whether or not they should have a pregnancy terminated. Anyone who knows anything about the Christian faith knows that whenever a human being takes on herself or himself an absolute right, there is something drastically wrong. This was the sin so graphically portrayed for us in the symbolic story of Gen., ch. 3—the attempt of human beings to be absolute centers of independent will. George H. Williams has put it this way:

> The ancient Roman *paterfamilias* had the right of life and death over the fetus within the womb of his wife; and not only could he sell his own child into slavery as its sire, but he could even in some circumstances lawfully put a son to death. To this day, according to Afghan law, it is the father who actually steps forward to execute the capital punishment decreed by the Muslim state, since the father is deemed the primary sovereign over his son whatever the age.

Horrible practices, we think. But Williams draws the appropriate conclusion with respect to abortion on demand:

Western civilization will have made no advance on this score if, in the present climate of sexual permissiveness amid ecological crisis, we accord now to the woman a prerogative that in the evolution of Western civilization was finally wrested from the omnipotent male.[57]

We are not in fact omnipotent creatures, but subjects of a sovereign Lord who requires that we live in loving relationship with him and our fellow human beings. When either one of those relationships is denied, and we become isolated centers of independent will, we are denying the very nature of our humanity.

To give another example in which modern women are inclined to absolutize themselves, many married women in the labor market now find themselves with paychecks in their pocketbooks. The difficulty is that some of them are not at all inclined to share those paychecks with their husbands. When it comes to spending money, they suddenly become very independent. They think it is their husbands' duty to support the family, but that the money they earn is "extra." Therefore they can spend it any way they please. They affirm their marital commitment and relationship, except in monetary matters, when they suddenly become little islands of will to themselves alone. I know several women whose husbands have no idea how much they earn, simply because they keep their wages secret in separate bank accounts. Such a denial of marital oneness in any area is foolish, but in money matters it is a threat to the very foundations of a home. Jesus tells us, "Where your treasure is, there will your heart be also" (Matt. 6:21). It is clear that the wife who cannot share her money with her husband is not likely to share her heart with him either.

Also, some modern so-called "liberated" women have absolutized themselves by being so concerned about their own rights that they have trampled over the rights of their husbands and children. There is nothing more tragic

affects of militant feminism on marriage

these days than those homes in which the marital relationship is being destroyed by feminist ideologies. The wife has suddenly realized that she is an "incomplete" or "unfulfilled" person. So she has precipitously rushed out and found a job, or is spending hours in women's meetings, or has abandoned all those little courtesies, amenities, and mutual services which make the life between a husband and wife possible. She has become an absolute center of self-assertion, with no regard for the welfare and feelings of her husband. Marriage is not possible under such circumstances, and it is not surprising that many of the militant feminists are also divorced. Some years ago, in an address to a symposium of eight hundred women at M.I.T., Alice Rossi even counseled such a course of action:

> If the marriage is not successful, the capable professional woman does not have to swallow hurt and pride and continue the marriage as many women do. For one reason, marriage has never been the exclusive center of her life; and secondly, she is perfectly competent to live and work on her own, and to seek and find a better relationship.[58]

It has been forgotten in such counsel that we shall find our lives only if we lose them (Mark 8:35 and pars.), and that that "better relationship" is had only in that mutual service and love to one another which is the imitation of Christ's service and love for us.

It is a significant phenomenon of the Biblical faith that we can search all through the pages of Scripture and find nothing about our rights, either our rights as human beings or our rights as men and women. Instead, the Bible talks only about our responsibilities—our responsibilities as sons and daughters of God. We have no rights, as far as the Biblical faith is concerned. We have no right to life—that is given us as a gift from our Creator. We have no right to happiness—that is a by-product of love and service. We have no right to forgiveness and love—

we deserve just the opposite. We have no right to our Christian freedom—Christ buys it for us with his blood. All that we have, all that we are, is given us as a gift from our Lord, and because he has given and given, we are responsible for using his gifts.

He has given us minds; he expects us to use them, by developing them to their full capacity for understanding and learning and for serving in his world. He has given us bodies; he expects us to honor them, and to keep them healthy and pure as the temples of his spirit. He has given us hearts; he expects us to love and to exercise forgiveness and compassion toward one another. He has given us strength; he expects us to work toward the fulfillment of his will, undergirding one another by our mutual labors in love. Indeed, the role of both men and women in this world is not to secure our own rights, but to use the gifts God in his mercy has given to us all—to pour out ourselves in service and work and compassion and caring, until there is shaped in this broken world of ours, homes that reflect the love of Christ and a society that allows entrance for the healing powers of the Kingdom of God.

It is possible, through faith in Jesus Christ, to heal the divisions between male and female that so disrupt our marriages. It is possible, in him, to be free and equal, and to exercise our total personhood. It is possible to live out that freedom and equality as whole and responsible men and women. But only through the life and death and resurrection of our Lord can we do all those things. The saying still holds for our marriages:

> Unless the LORD builds the house,
> those who build it labor in vain.
> (Ps. 127:1.)

CHAPTER 6

Marriage
as Discipleship

If any one says, "I love God," and hates his brother, he is a liar; for he who does not love his brother whom he has seen, cannot love God whom he has not seen.—I John 4:20

In the adventure of trying to live a Christian life, it is fully as important to work at improving our marriages as it is to pray or to study the Bible or to go to church. The latter disciplines have always been considered necessities for Christian living—and they are! But marriage too is a discipleship and should receive fully as much attention and care from the devout as does the life of prayer and meditation.

Some churches have been slow to recognize this. Most congregations have Bible study groups of one sort or another, meeting regularly, and that is good. But not too many congregations have organized ongoing marital enrichment groups. Almost every preacher emphasizes the life of prayer and devotion, but few deliver sermons on married life, except perhaps on Mother's Day. Even among Bible scholars and church leaders, Biblical research continues apace, but it is accompanied by an ever-increasing divorce rate among such clergy. Some church leaders who would vehemently insist that social justice in race relations, for example, is a *sine qua non* for the Christian, nevertheless systematically isolate their families from their Christian purview by neglecting them to attend "important meetings" most days of the year.

In our Christian understanding and practice there is a neat separation made between marriage and discipleship, between what we owe to God and what we do to our spouses and children. Only when a shocking situation arises do we sense the relationship between them, as for example when a former minister of ours deserted his wife and four children and ran off with the female Sunday school superintendent. The congregation was sure that it was an act inconsistent with the Christian life, but they never could fully agree on just why that was so! Neither will many of the readers of this book. Marriage some-how, for many of us, is in a realm apart from religion. There are those who believe that it is perfectly possible to be a Christian and at the same time be at odds with one's spouse. Sad to say, that is the state of thousands of Christians in church every Sunday morning.

Let us therefore briefly look back over the path we have come in the previous chapters in order to emphasize the nature of Christian marriage as discipleship. Thereby perhaps we will be able to bridge the chasm that so many have attempted to dig between what we do in our living rooms and what we do in our religious sanctuaries.

Up to this point, I have presented the basic characteris-tics of Christian marriage and the roles of free and equal Christian men and women in it. We have seen that actually Christian marriage is marked by a double com-mitment. There is the total, accepting, exclusive, continu-ing, growing, anticipating commitment of husband and wife to one another. Beyond that, there is the commit-ment of both partners to Jesus Christ. In Christian marriage, the first commitment really rests upon the second. Indeed, without the commitment of the couple to Christ, their commitment to each other loses its most powerful support.

Christian couples are called into marriage as part of their Christian vocation, because they are convinced that it is the will of God that their lives be joined in lifelong communion. Psychologists tell us that each of us could probably have achieved a happy marriage with any one of a number of possible mates, but for those faithful who achieve continuing marital harmony, their union seems divinely willed. They are deeply convinced that they were destined for and guided to each other "from the foundation of the earth." Be that as it may, the choice of a mate confronts the sincere Christian with a question about God, with the question as to whether or not his or her commitment to Christ can be carried out in union with the chosen life partner.

It is this prior commitment to the will of God as revealed by Jesus Christ that is recognized, not only in the Christian marriage vows but also in the teaching of the gospel. Jesus tells his disciples, "What therefore God has joined together, let not man put asunder" (Mark 10:9 and par.). Our Lord assumes that God wills specific marital union, and every Christian asks himself or herself, before marriage, if he or she is choosing in concert with that divine will. The marriage vow, then, affirms that such is the case:

> I, (name), take thee, (name), to be my wedded wife/husband, to have and to hold from this day forward, for better for worse, for richer for poorer, in sickness and in health, to love and to cherish, till death us do part, *according to God's holy ordinance;* and thereto I give thee my pledge.

The presupposition here is that the specific marriage taking place is according to God's ordering of his universe and that he is actively working within the marriage to further his good purpose for his world. To enter sincerely into such a vow, the Christian must first have committed himself or herself to God, and the commitment to the marriage partner grows out of that prior dedication. The very act of getting married is understood as an act of discipleship!

The Christian marital relation, then, is modeled upon Christ's love for his church. Husband and wife are to love each other as Christ has loved them. That has always been the nature of Christian discipleship—the thankful response to God's act toward us in Jesus Christ, in a life of serving and caring patterned after the life of Christ.

> A new commandment I give to you, that you love one another; even as I have loved you, that you also love one another. By this all men will know that you are my disciples, if you have love for one another. (John 13:34–35.)

We have not often recognized it, but that commandment applies to marriage also. It is in the marital relation, as well as in our other relations with our fellow human beings, that our Christian discipleship is lived out. There, in the ways we act toward our spouses, in how we view them and live with them, we write the story of our faithful or unfaithful discipleship.

This was long ago recognized by the prophet Malachi. The Jews languished in a ruined Jerusalem, shortly before the reforms of Nehemiah (ca. 450 B.C.), and moaned in their poverty and hopelessness that God had forgotten them. Malachi pointed out that their faithlessness toward God was clearly manifested in the faithlessness of their marriages. Their present suffering had direct relation to what they were doing in their homes:

> You cover the LORD's altar with tears, with weeping and groaning because he no longer regards the offering or accepts it with favor at your hand. You ask, "Why does he not?" Because the LORD was witness to the covenant between you and the wife of your youth, to whom you have been faithless,

though she is your companion and your wife by covenant.
(Mal. 2:13–14.)

The Lord is the witness to the covenant between Christian husband and wife! As with that passage in Eph., ch. 5, which we discussed in Chapter 5, what we do to our mates in our marriages, we do also to the Lord. Christian commitment and marital commitment are two sides of one dedication.

We have also seen that it is because of our commitment to Christ that we are able to grant one another in marriage full equality, personhood, and freedom. It is in Christ that the brokenness of the relationship between male and female is overcome, and the possibility of joyful equality and unity between husband and wife is restored. It is in Christ that we see the true picture of humanity as it was meant to be. It is to Christ that husband and wife are called to give the full response of personhood, loving the God revealed in Jesus Christ with all their hearts and souls and minds and strength, in the full exercise of their God-given personalities. Christian discipleship therefore involves granting full personhood and equality to each other in marriage, living out the true humanity and freedom that Christ has made possible to us.

To put it in words that Paul uses in I Cor., ch. 12, God has given us each a gift of the Spirit, and Christian discipleship becomes a matter of exercising that gift fully, of allowing each other in marriage to be all that God intended, of not hindering the freedom of our spouses in Christ to become what God intends.

> "What no eye has seen, nor ear heard,
> nor the heart of man conceived,
> what God has prepared for those who love,"
> God has revealed to us through the Spirit. (I Cor. 2:9–10.)

There opens before the Christian husband and wife the vista of marvelous adventure, the task of pressing "on toward the goal for the prize of the upward call of God in Christ Jesus" (Phil. 3:14). Christian discipleship involves, in marriage, the freedom to pursue that task, and the joy of knowing that one pursues it in company with another beloved disciple.

Should not we Christians, in our broken world, become acutely aware therefore that there is more at stake in our marriages than merely our own personal happiness or that of our children? God knows that these factors in themselves are important enough—especially the health and wholeness of our beloved children, whom our marital relations so deeply affect! But there is more involved than even our children's lives or our own. We have to do with God in Christ, at our breakfast tables and in our bedrooms. All the daily little routines of marriage are pieces of our love or indifference toward him. To paraphrase I John 4:20, "If any one says, 'I love God,' and hates his spouse, he is a liar; for he who does not love his spouse whom he has seen, cannot love God whom he has not seen." It is in relation to each other in our homes that the nature of our discipleship is manifested, and if we fail each other in marriage, we fail our Lord Jesus Christ. We say, in effect, as Peter in his denial, "I do not know the man" (Matt. 26:72 and pars.). We deny our commitment to our God when we fail to live out our marital commitment.

Such thoughts, of course, make some "marriage experts" cringe in horror. Some of them have worked for years to free marriage from all its "idealistic" baggage. They want to get men and women to view it "realistically" in terms of desires and compatibilities, to convince the world that marital harmony has to do with psychological and sociological and physical needs, which must be satisfied if the marriage is to be successful. Thus we now have scores of marriage manuals full of the proper techniques for sex or communication or "fighting fairly" within marriage. I do not want to underestimate the value of some of the insights contained in such manuals. I incorporate many of them in this book and am indebted to them.

Nevertheless, we human beings are not alone on this earth, or in our flights beyond it. We inhabit our universe with a Lord who has promised to be with us always. He encompasses us about though we take the wings of the morning or dwell in the uttermost parts of the sea, he has knit us together in our mothers' wombs and planned the days of our lives, he is there in our darkness and in the depths, as he is in our brightest heavens, and discerns our thoughts and knows our ways and searches us altogether (Ps. 139). We are made by that Lord and responsible to him and have the purpose of our living from him, and we cannot pretend that what we do has only to do with ourselves.

We were not made to copulate like irresponsible animals, nor to function autonomously like self-contained centers of mechanistic desires. When we fulfill only ourselves we deny our very nature, and reduce the glory of human life to naturalistic needs, self-serving, grubbily transitory, and violently aggressive. It is that sterile vision of our lives which has reduced sex to cold technique, and human community to psychological manipulation, and love to a passing satisfaction of a need for personal fulfillment. Our society cries out and groans in travail under the burden of a humanity deprived of its responsibility to God, and voices such as Karl Menninger's plead for a new understanding of our relation to some divine dimension.[59] Human life above all else has to do first with God. Marital partners who do not live that fact really have no possibility of being fully human.

Christians therefore bear a double responsibility in their marriages—a responsibility to themselves and each other, and a responsibility to God. It is neither kindness nor scientific "progress" to try to relieve them of that fact. Like Job, we might feel more comfortable if God left us alone long enough to swallow our spittle (Job 7:19), but then human life might really be nothing more than sorrow and wounds and suffering on an ash heap, with no point whatsoever. Who really wants to continue in that kind of life? Not Job! Certainly not we!

Let all who would relieve us of the burden of the Christian yoke of responsibility (Matt. 11:28–30)—all the well-meaning psychiatrists and sociologists and marriage experts—let them all leave us Christians to wrestle with our God and our cross-haunted consciences and our seemingly outdated morality. It may be the only ray of hope on the marital horizon of our troubled society.

Jesus once told his disciples that we are the "light of the world," and that we should not try to be like other people, hiding our light under convention's bushels, but rather that we should put our lamp on a stand and let it give "light to all in the house" (Matt. 5:14–15). Could it be that that is finally the task of Christian marriage? Is it not only a lifelong vocation in which we wrestle and grow and learn and fight for our commitment to God and to each other, but is it also to be a light shining into the darkness of our society's homes? David Mace once wrote:

> By their gracious influence, Christian homes win more converts than all the preachers put together. Give us enough of them, and the world would soon be a Christian world; for the world's life rises to higher levels only as its homes do so.[60]

We Christians finally bear witness to the world by how we live out our marital commitments. By the way we spouses get along with each other and with our children, we tell our agonized society that there is hope of healing for its grievous wounds, or we announce that the patient has the "sickness unto death" and that there is no possibility of recovery. By the way we conduct our marriages, we proclaim that Jesus Christ has won the victory over sin in the marital sphere too, or we confess that he is powerless to reconcile husband and wife, parents and children, old folks and youth.

I believe that there is good news for our nation's homes. I believe that the light has shone in the darkness, and the darkness has not put it out. The widespread disintegration of the American home need not be accepted as inevitable, for in the cross and resurrection of Jesus Christ is the healing for all our private hells.

I also know that we Christians have daily work to do, and that most of that work must take place within the spheres of our private lives. There, concretely, slowly, sometimes painfully, we must work out our commitment and our discipleship, in our relations with the husbands or wives whom God has given us. Christian marriage, the committed marriage, is not trouble free and easy. But by the grace of God in Jesus Christ, it is a real possibility.

CHAPTER 7

Is the Tie
Blessed That Binds?

Every one then who hears these words of mine and does them will be like a wise man who built his house upon the rock; and the rain fell, and the floods came, and the winds blew and beat upon that house, but it did not fall, because it had been founded on the rock.—Matt. 7:24–25

One of the major tasks that a Christian marriage partner has in living out his or her marital commitment is that of constancy. We have described the Christian marriage as one characterized by total and exclusive commitment to each other in a lifelong, continuing, and growing relationship. No understanding of marriage is under more severe attack these days than is this Christian conviction as to the necessity of faithfulness in marriage. Not only have studies such as those of Kinsey revealed that extramarital relations are prevalent throughout our culture, but cultural expectations and mores have now changed. There is little community disapproval of extramarital affairs, pregnancies out of wedlock, and divorce. One has only to tune in to the television soap operas on any afternoon to find that faithfulness in marriage is largely an expectation of the past and that the central sympathetic roles in television dramas portray divorcées, adulterers, fornicators, and unwed parents—if I may be permitted those strong and now seldom-used terms. Christian spouses are surrounded on every side in our culture by those who violate their marital vows, and they must learn how to come to terms with such non-Christian influences.

Most insidious in their negative influence upon Christian constancy are those marriage "experts," who maintain that faithfulness may in fact be bad for a marriage. Carl Rogers, in his book *Becoming Partners*, has not gone quite that far: we quoted his findings on the drawbacks of communal sex in Chapter 3.[61] Nevertheless there can be no doubt that the real heroes of marriage for Rogers are those young couples who have left behind all traditional and religious codes of morality in order to experiment with every type of sexual and marital behavior. He feels that "to give them their old-fashioned names, 'living in sin,' 'committing adultery,' 'lewd and lascivious conduct,' 'fornication,' 'homosexuality,' 'ingesting illegal drugs,' even 'soliciting' " is "frankly ridiculous." "Perhaps one thing we as a culture might do," he writes, "which would preserve this enormously valuable laboratory, these pioneering ventures into new relationship space, would be to relieve them of the ever-present shadow of moral reproach and criminal action." This would, Rogers feels, "be an enormous step forward in facing reality" which would "set the stage for a partnership revolution, a relationship revolution." [62] Such is Rogers' pioneer call to young Americans!

More insidious because more subtle is the widely read work of Nena and George O'Neill, entitled *Open Marriage: A New Life Style for Couples*.[63] In that work, the O'Neills contrast what they imagine to be bad "closed marriage" with good "open marriage." They list as "unrealistic expectations, unreasonable ideals, and mythological beliefs of closed marriage" the following: that it will last forever; that it means total commitment; that it will bring happiness, comfort, and security; that fidelity is a true measure of the love you have for each other; that your mate will definitely be the parent of your child. "Every single one of these ideals, beliefs or expectations is false in one way or another," write the O'Neills, "and practically impossible to attain, much less to sustain. . . . Any of them that you do manage to make come true, unfortunately, are almost certain to be at the cost of personal freedom and individual development, with consequent damage to children and to the overall success of the marriage itself." [64] If we want successful marriages, we should, according to the O'Neills, give up all thought of lifelong and total commitment to each other. Those may be the very things that will harm our marriage!

With regard to sexual relations, the O'Neills state that the question must be seriously raised whether or not sexual monogamy provides a realistic or viable standard in a society so diverse and changing as ours. The O'Neills are sure that partners to a marriage should have free and open relationships with those outside the marriage, and that those relationships may include sex:

> If partners in an open marriage do have outside sexual relationships, it is on the basis of their own internal relationship—that is, because they have experienced mature love, have real trust, and are able to expand themselves, to love and enjoy others and to bring that love and pleasure back into their marriage, without jealousy.[65]

Partners should not deceive each other about their outside relationships, maintain the O'Neills, and they should engage in such freedom only when it brings individual growth and the growth of one's partner.[66]

In short, what the O'Neills are implying is that truly

mature and ideal couples are those who have been able to leave behind them the confining commitments of Christian marriage for the wide open spaces of self-fulfillment and development. How deceptively attractive and temptingly superior they try to make such marriage sound! How easily the practitioner of the "open marriage" would be able to scoff at the supposedly "closed" understanding of the Christian marriage! Such are the assaults on their commitment that Christian couples have to face in our society.

It may be somewhat comforting for Christians to know that many other marital counselors disagree with the views of *Open Marriage*. For example, Dr. George R. Bach, the founder and director of the Institute of Group Psychotherapy in Beverly Hills, California, who has wide experience in counseling with thousands of couples, has stated, "For real intimates infidelity tends to pall."

> . . . to the detriment of further growth of the motel industry, our most sexually mature adults, perhaps after a period of extracurricular experimentation, do not enjoy being adulterers. It is simply not a rewarding role in the long run. This is why so many mistresses of married men lose out in the end. The men may claim they cannot leave their wives "for the children's sakes." If they were honest with themselves and their extracurricular ladies, most of these husbands would probably confess that it is not so much the children who tie down wandering males but the comforts of making love to "the one and only." [67]

There is a dependable structure, based on our commitment to one another, which is necessary for the growth of the human personality as it has been created by God. We need intimacy, we need love, we need opportunities to give and to be needed, we need recognition for what we achieve and are, and acceptance and understanding. We need outlets for the pleasure which our senses and bodies can bring to us; we need to feel worthwhile and worthy.

There is no relation that more pleasurably and adequately meets those needs than does the relationship of the committed marriage.[68] Edward Carpenter has put it this way:

> That there should exist one other person in the world toward whom all openness of exchange should establish itself, from whom there should be no concealment; whose body should be as dear to one, in every part, as one's own; with whom there should be no sense of mine or thine, in property or possession; into whose mind one's thoughts should naturally flow, as it were to know themselves and receive a new illumination; and between whom and oneself there should be a spontaneous rebound of sympathy in all the joys and sorrows and experiences of life; such is perhaps one of the dearest wishes of the soul.[69]

It is in the truly committed marriage that such "dearest wishes of the soul" are realized, and apart from such commitment they are impossible of achievement.

We need to look further, however, at the nature of such commitment. What is it finally that holds the Christian marriage together? What is the blessed tie that binds, through all the heights and depths and seasons of wedlock? Where is that firm foundation on which we can erect a home, that rock which remains immovable though all the waters of our world's chaos and infidelity beat and rage against it (Matt. 7:24–27 and par.)?

Jesus tells us that the firm foundation for all our actions, the one that cannot be shaken, is the hearing and doing of his words (Matt. 7:24). That applies also to marriage. Therefore we need to know two things. We need to know just what the teaching of our Lord and of the Bible is with regard to marital fidelity. And we need to know how to understand and apply that teaching.

There is very little compromise with respect to divorce and infidelity in the Scriptures. The ancient law of Deut. 24:1–4 allowed a husband to divorce his wife very easily, but it is countermanded in both the Old Testament and the New. To look again at Mal. 2:13 ff., that passage assumes that life and godly offspring are possible only in the united home:

> Has not the one God made and sustained for us the spirit of life? And what does he desire? Godly offspring. So take heed to yourselves, and let none be faithless to the wife of his youth. "For I hate divorce," says the LORD the God of Israel, and covering one's garment with violence, says the LORD of hosts. So take heed to yourselves and do not be faithless." (Mal. 2:15–16.)

Deuteronomy 24:1–4 is specifically reinterpreted by Jesus in his teaching. According to Mark 10:1–12 and its parallel in Matt. 19:1–9 (cf. Luke 16:18), Jesus said the law of divorce in Deuteronomy was given man because of his "hardness of heart," that is, because of his sin. Man's sinful rebellion against God had made divorce necessary. However, Jesus changed the law by stating that "from the beginning it was not so" (Matt. 19:8), that is, from the time of creation on. God did not intend divorce to be a part of his good creation. Instead,

> "God made them male and female." "For this reason a man shall leave his father and mother and be joined to his wife, and the two shall become one." So they are no longer two but one. What therefore God has joined together, let not man put asunder. (Mark 10:6–9.)

So indissoluble is the marriage union, according to Jesus, that he adds these words, when the disciples ask him privately about the matter:

> Whoever divorces his wife and marries another, commits adultery against her; and if she divorces her husband and marries another, she commits adultery. (Mark 10:11–12.)

The full force of such words is felt when we realize that adultery is specifically forbidden in the Ten Commandments (Ex. 20:14; Deut. 5:18) and judged by Jesus himself to be an offense worthy to be punished in hell (Matt. 5:27–30). To be sure, both Matt. 5:32 and 19:9 give evidence of a softening of Jesus' statement by allowing divorce on the grounds of unchastity. Nevertheless in the older more original tradition Jesus' opposition to the separation of husband and wife, as an act at odds with the will of God, is made clear.

Paul apparently accepted as genuine the tradition of Jesus' rejection of divorce, since Paul stated that it is a specific command from the Lord

> that the wife should not separate from her husband (but if she does, let her remain single or else be reconciled to her husband)—and that the husband should not divorce his wife. (I Cor. 7:10–11.)

Paul then added his own words to this command, in I Cor. 7:12–16, stating that those who were married to unbelievers also should not separate, since the believing spouse might consecrate and bring the unbeliever to Christ. In short, both Old Testament and New strictly forbid divorce to the people of God.

In even stricter fashion, adultery is always prohibited. The fact that its prohibition was included in the Decalogue means that it was viewed as antithetical to the basic intention of God. The Decalogue sets forth in summary fashion only those things which were absolutely forbidden to the covenant people, those acts which would immediately place their perpetrators outside of the grace of God. Adultery stands as one of that basic list of absolutely fobidden acts (cf. Jer. 7:9 ff.; Rom. 2:22; James 2:11). In Deut. 22:22–24 and Lev. 20:10, the punishment for adultery is death, and throughout the Bible, it is viewed in the most serious terms. According to Jesus' words, it is not merely an outward physical act, but also a corruption within man's inner self (Matt. 15:19; cf. ch. 5:28). In The Psalms, it is a violation of faith and knowledge which violates man's total self, and which therefore makes it impossible for him to participate in fellowship with God (Ps. 50:16–18). Paul says that adulterers cannot inherit the Kingdom of God (I Cor. 6:9; cf. I Thess. 4:3–8). Other writers are sure that adulterers stand under judgment (Mal. 3:5; Heb. 13:4) and bring God's curse on all their land (Jer. 23:10), causing those who have traffic with them to forfeit their very lives (Prov. 6:26). There is no passage in which adultery is excused or overlooked because of mitigating circumstances.

Paul also states, in a passage often overlooked, that to love one's neighbor as oneself is to fulfill the commandment prohibiting adultery (Rom. 13:8–10). That is, one's spouse is one's nearest and dearest neighbor, and love for that "neighbor," in the manner of Christ's love, makes adultery impossible.

So there is no room in the Biblical faith for marital infidelity or inconstancy. The conjugal union is regarded as a lifelong commitment, willed and protected by God himself, and those who violate that union are considered to stand under the most serious divine judgment. Any Christian mate who takes the teaching of the Bible seriously has to regard divorce and adultery as among the most serious sins.

How does the Christian apply that teaching in his or her own marriage in the twentieth century? Jesus taught us that the hearing and doing of his words would give us a firm foundation for living our lives, but are his words to be regarded as some sort of law, as some sort of legal literalistic stricture? Even literalists are very selective in the words to which they adhere as norms. Can we, as Christians, assume that once married, we are married for life and therefore need not worry any more about the question?

The difficulty is that too many Christians have in past

times so regarded themselves in marriage. They have assumed in legalistic fashion that divorce is wrong, that infidelity is not to be tolerated, that their marriages are "forever." So they have made very little effort to work at their wedded unions, to improve their relations with their mates over the span of a lifetime, to keep their love growing and deepening through all changes and difficulties. It is these couples who have settled down into a routine of mutual boredom and suppressed hostility. They really have no experience of the joy and vitality that are intended to accompany Christian wedlock. We have all seen such couples at some time, perhaps in a restaurant. They eat a whole meal together without exchanging a word. They look idly about, in bored resignation, rarely taking any notice of each other except to pass the salt. It is clear that they find nothing new about each other and have ceased to look for it. Their marriages are taken for granted, as is their routine life in general. Little disturbs the slogging pace of just one day after another. Such couples are vivid illustration that "the written code kills, but the Spirit gives life" (II Cor. 3:6). When we change the good news of the gospel into law, it is unable to give us life.

No law, either religious or civil, ever held a marriage together in any acceptable fashion. This is not to say that there should be no law with respect to marriage. As in every area, the law in wedlock acts as a check on sin—a point that situation ethics often overlooks, when it maintains that all actions should be based simply on the decision of love in the light of the circumstances. Certainly the commandment forbidding adultery has prevented some unfaithfulness, and the Christian marriage vows have held together some couples who would otherwise have separated.

In a study of divorce,[70] Dr. Jessie Bernard has shown that a divorce undertaken by a wife is seldom an impulsive act, and that it usually takes her about seven months to make up her mind and file a suit. During this period, the wife is under great stress, and Dr. Bernard states, "It could be argued that if these women knew with certainty that they could not have a divorce, that this solution to their problem was impossible, . . . they would learn to live with their marriages without too great difficulty." In such cases, a law forbidding divorce serves a useful and preventive function. But "learning to live with a marriage" and making it vital and joyful are two different things. While a law may hold sin in check, it cannot overcome it.

We should be grateful for the law. We all have known times in our marriages when they were held together by nothing more than duty, and that obligation to a legalistic expectation has prevented us from doing some foolish things that we undoubtedly would have grievously regretted later. When temptation threatens, as it does in every marriage, it is good to know in the back of our minds that stern and divine, "Thou shall not . . . !" As Paul puts it, "the law was our custodian until Christ came" (Gal. 3:24). But the law is negative: it can prevent; it has little power to create.

Joyful marriages are never built on codes and legalistic "contracts" alone. Those so-called "modern" couples, who are actually writing out detailed contracts specifying their respective duties (she does the housework on Tuesdays, Thursdays, and Saturdays, he on the other days), should keep this fact in mind. As Jesus put it, "When you have done all that is commanded you, say, 'We are unworthy servants; we have only done what was our duty' " (Luke 17:10)—we have not earned either abundant life or blissful wedded unions. Marriage must be built on a much different rock from that of legalism.

Some persons try to preserve their marriages by even more uncertain guarantees. Some count on social convention to keep their mates faithful to them ("I hope you realize how foolish you looked last night, flirting with that divorcée at the party"). But our society is pulling this support from under them. Only a few groups, such as politicians and religious leaders, now worry about the "image" that divorce might give them. Other couples keep their marriages together for the sake of the children. Usually such unions fail as soon as the children have grown and left home. Some rely on economics—it is so expensive to get a divorce—or on the fact that it is more convenient and comfortable to be married than it is to be single. Tragically, many think to hold their mates by physical attraction alone. Waging a desperate battle against gray hairs and wrinkles, bulges and muscle aches, sagging skin and fatigue, the cosmetic industry prospers, but the marriage fails. Love realistically accepts the passing years, or it is not love at all.

Perhaps most subtly deceptive is the common argument of the psychologists that marriages endure when the union effectively meets the respective needs of the partners. Certainly this is true from one perspective. Any marriage that does not at least partially fulfill our "heart hungers" for security and independence, for acceptance and love, for physical and emotional satisfaction, for valuation of ourselves as human, is in for a great deal of rough going and trouble. The fallacy of basing the permanence of a union on mutual fulfillment of needs alone, however, is illustrated very simply in the following conversation:

He: Honey, don't be upset. You know I've never found anyone who better meets all my needs than you do.
She (*tearfully*): But what if you did?

On that latter question alone many marriages have foundered. Men have found others who have "understood" them better than have their wives, and in middle age, have left behind home and children for that greater understanding. Women have been introduced to males who have made them feel more "important" and "self-sufficient" than have their patronizing husbands and have left behind housework and P.T.A. for roles that seemed more adventurous. It is important that our needs in marriage be met, but if that is all that holds our unions together, then they will crumble as soon as someone or something else better fulfills those needs. Women entering the liberation movement and shortly after applying for divorce illustrate the point.

Marriage, through all its vicissitudes, conflicts, and changes, can only certainly endure if it rests upon the firm rock of inner faith and conviction. Jesus tells us that divorce and infidelity are wrong, that God wants our marriages to last a lifetime. My marriage will endure only if my husband and I believe those teachings with all our hearts, souls, minds, and strength, and consequently are willing to work long and hard to make our marriage enduring.

Moreover, we believe those teachings of our Lord, not because they are some law laid upon us, but because we trust the goodness and purpose of the One who gives them to us. We trust God: we trust that he loves us, that he wants us to have life and to have it more abundantly, that he has sent his Son to reveal how to have that life and to make it possible, that through all the events of our lives he is present with us and working out his good purpose for us. We therefore also trust those things he has told us in his word. We trust that his teachings are for our good, that they will in fact lead us in the path of full and joyful living. "These things I have spoken to you," Jesus said, "that my joy may be in you, and that your joy may be full." (John 15:11.) And that which Jesus has spoken to us concerning our marriages is his command to be faithful: "What therefore God has joined together, let not man put asunder" (Mark 10:9).

We entered our marriage in the Christian conviction that it was the will of God. Therefore we struggle and work and persevere in preserving our marriage, because we are deeply and inwardly convinced that that too is the will of God, and that his will lights the path which alone leads to life and good. We believe that God will support and help us to preserve our marriage, but we also know that we ourselves must daily work to live out our inner convictions. We will be no less tempted than are other couples; our conflicts and troubles will be no fewer. But we build on the firm rock of trust in God and his Son, of hearing Jesus' words and doing them, and we therefore become like that man in Jesus' teaching

> who built his house upon the rock; and the rain fell, and the floods came, and the winds blew and beat upon that house, but it did not fall, because it had been founded on the rock. (Matt. 7:24–25.)

Many things are involved in hearing and doing Jesus' words in marriage, in working to preserve our unions and thereby acting out our convictions. Chief among them are our constant efforts to communicate openly with each other and to conquer and learn from the conflicts that we inevitably will have with the other. We will discuss those topics in the chapters that follow. But surely the first prerequisite for marital fidelity is letting our partner know that he or she is at the center of our hearts, that he or she is the most important person in our lives and will always so be treated. It is important to tell our mate in words, every day through the years, that he or she is our most intimate and valued companion and will never be replaced, no matter how attractive or understanding or compatible some other acquaintance may be. It is important that our mates see that we will never enter into other relationships that would destroy the intimacy we have with them.

Intimacy in marriage takes many forms. It is not only

sexual, but also emotional, intellectual, aesthetic. It comes from values shared and work done together. It is deepened by crises faced and overcome in partnership. It grows out of creative achievements to which both spouses have contributed—the raising of children, the decorating of a home, the planting of a garden. It is spawned by mutual dreams realized and common fun enjoyed. It can come from both harmony and conflict, if they are rightly shared.

Of course we do and should share with other people. We work and play, discuss and argue, grieve and rejoice with friends and colleagues. No healthy home can live in isolation from the rest of the world. In God's world we are all members of one body, fellow members of the household of faith and of the family of humankind. We are to be involved with other people's lives, to "rejoice with those who rejoice" and "weep with those who weep" (Rom. 12:15).

Yet, other persons are not to occupy the central place in our hearts. That is reserved for the nearest and dearest of our neighbors, the beloved spouse with whom we are joined in the unity of one flesh by God. It is important for our mates to know that they have that reserved spot, that we will never let ourselves continue in some experience with another which would replace our primary loyalty to our mates. Only if our mates realize in the depths of their hearts that they remain number one in our lives are they given the security and freedom to live creatively and joyfully. Jealousy never helps a marriage; it only destroys it. Perfect love "casts out fear" (I John 4:18), and only those who feel secure because they are loved are able fully to be themselves, to be free really to become the persons God intended them to be.

On this score, there is no character trait more typical of the Christian than that of dependability. When I think about my own children's marriages in the coming years, I am inclined to believe that nothing is more central to their happiness than that they marry truly Christian persons. By Christian I do not mean the common run of church-goers, the nominal adherents who really do not know what it means to be dedicated to Jesus Christ. I mean those faithful ones who, through weeks and months and years of disciplined practice in prayer and study and worship, have absorbed the word of God into their bones and have come to know the presence of God with them as a constant reality. I would like my children to marry persons on the way to becoming *that* kind of Christian.

We do not meet such persons too often, though they are present in almost every Christian congregation and in almost every church institution such as a seminary. And they can be picked out like gleaming lights in the darkness. They are persons on whom one can depend, persons whom one knows will always try to do the right thing, *as that right is defined in the Scriptures' witness.* They are persons who have known the mercy of God and who therefore show it to others, who insist on justice and forgiveness and concern for other persons, who walk in humility and gentleness and compassion and who resist in themselves the ways of pride and violence and indifference. Such Christians, in their own marriages, exhibit a dependable fidelity, which one knows instinctively could not be overcome by all the powers of hell. In that fidelity, they are indeed "the salt of the earth" (Matt. 5:13) and "the light of the world" (Matt. 5:14). They put to shame, by their constancy, all those who are unfaithful, because they stand as incontrovertible witnesses to the possibility of Christian marriage, the highest form of communion between a man and woman on this earth.

It follows then that part of working out our lifelong commitment to our mates involves the practice of our own Christian discipline of prayer and Bible study and attendance at worship. Those disciplines alone increase our trust in God and our faithfulness to his will. We come to know God only in the Word and Sacraments through which he has chosen to reveal himself to us. There really is no other way. Jesus told us that long ago. "I am the way, and the truth, and the life," he said; "no one comes to the Father, but by me." (John 14:6.) While that may seem offensive to many casual practitioners of "religion," it nevertheless is the narrow gateway which leads to life (cf. Matt. 7:13–14). We may dabble in our mystic religions and consult our horoscopes and listen to our gurus in our dalliance with the ultimate. When the decision truly is made to seek the abundant life, the wise turn to Jesus Christ and take his way and truth seriously, shouldering that yoke of Christian discipline apart from which none of us can know the Father.

Christian marriages blossom and bloom in the good earth of lively communion with God. In the psalmist's picture (Ps. 1), they become like trees "planted by streams of water," yielding their fruit and not withering, no matter that ill winds blow against them. Part of the responsibility of marriage, therefore, is always seeking that "living water" (cf. John 4:10; Jer. 2:13) by the constant practice of prayer and worship and study of the Scriptures. Temple Gairdner put it this way in a profound prayer recorded in his diary before his marriage:

> That I may come near to her, draw me nearer to Thee than to her; that I may know her, make me to know Thee more than her; that I may love her with the perfect love of a perfectly whole heart, cause me to love Thee more than her and most of all.
> That nothing may be between me and her, be Thou between us, every moment. That we may be constantly together, draw us into separate loneliness with Thyself. And when we meet breast to breast, O God, let it be upon Thine own.[71]

The Christian who trusts God and who seeks to realize God's will for his or her marriage is not immune to the trials and sufferings to which faith is subject. There are times also in Christian marriage when we must believe even when we cannot see, when we must cling to the conviction that God wills our union though all the evidence seems to the contrary, when we must proceed on sheer faith alone, crying out with that desperate cry, "I believe; help my unbelief!" (Mark 9:24).

The Christian faith often operates with a lack of evidence that seems ridiculous to the rest of the world. It often seems to contradict the plain facts with a foolhardy "nevertheless." Such foolhardiness is built into our faith, because we proceed on the irrational assumption that God the Son has become a man among us, and we stake our lives on nothing but the story of the crucifixion and resurrection of that Son. In the darkest moments of life, when God seems totally absent, we claim that he is nevertheless present and at work. When all happiness and good seem lost, we maintain that nevertheless the Kingdom is coming. We entertain the seemingly ridiculous notions that nothing can separate us from the love of God, that he is working out a good purpose for us even when we are suffering or in pain, that he cares so much that he has numbered the very hairs of our heads, that the sovereign Ruler of the universe marks our every individual moment. Foolish? Yes indeed it is foolish, but nevertheless true. It is the one truth that makes any sense when life collapses in upon us, when all is inner pain and suffering, and there seems no way out, when human beings, including ourselves, seem nothing but false and deceptive, and joy and love appear to be goods of the past which we shall never know again. God has come among us in Jesus Christ, and now remains in our midst by his Spirit, working out a good purpose of love for us and those we hold dear. That is the one fact that makes any sense in our chaotic and tortured world, and it is to that fact which we cling in our marriages, even in those times when they seem to us to be hell.

Suppose, however, that a union seems incapable of

improvement. How long should anyone who holds such faith endure? Unfortunately Christians often find themselves wedded to persons who do not share their convictions, and they find that they alone are carrying the full burden of fidelity to the marriage, or that they alone are exerting effort to improve the relationship. It is almost impossible to heal a marriage under such circumstances, and the Christian who continues for an extended length of time in such a relationship often suffers a kind of martyrdom. Is the Christian spouse obligated to remain in a marriage in which the partner is an alcoholic who will not seek help, or is repeatedly adulterous, or is mentally or physically cruel? What exactly are the Christian limits of fidelity? Is there no time when divorce is appropriate for the follower of Christ?

There are no general answers which can be given to such questions. Certainly there are situations in which separation or divorce seems the only way out. The apostle Paul recognizes the validity of the problems involved (I Cor. 7:12–16), and the continuance of some marriages would seem like a denial of the mercy of Christ himself, the condemnation of a suffering soul to unbearable torment. I think, for example, of the man who discovered after his marriage that his wife had only pretended love, when in fact she was after the money she thought he would inherit. Because the man was a deeply committed Christian, he tried for twenty-five years to heal the union. For long stretches of time he suffered total physical rejection from his wife, even being spat upon and forced for months to cook his own food and to eat apart at another table. The man held out in the relationship until the two children it produced were grown; he then finally divorced the wife and subsequently remarried. Those of us who knew of his trials could only wonder why he had not filed for divorce years before. Yet, when he finally took the step, he did so with the knowledge that he had believed and loved to the uttermost limits of his being. Who can say that he should have initiated divorce proceedings earlier?

To give a personal witness, I grew up in a home which, for a period, was marked by violent differences, arguments, and the threat of divorce. Through all the turbulence and heartache, my Christian mother refused to agree to the separation because she thought it was wrong for a Christian to do so. Some outside of the family thought she was foolish, but personally I am deeply grateful to her. Contrary to the belief of some psychologists, she prevented psychic damage to her children far beyond what measure of it we suffered in the troubled home. She lived to enjoy a mellowed and loving relationship with Dad in their later years. He himself came to a simple but deep Christian faith, and the last words I heard Mother say to him before her death were, "You really do love me, don't you?" As Paul puts it, "The unbelieving husband is consecrated through his wife" (I Cor. 7:14). There are times, in truth, in which persistent faith does produce miracles, and it seems as if we Christians sometimes have to wrestle and be wounded and hang on and refuse to let go, clinging to our marriage unions and crying out, like Jacob, "I will not let you go, unless you bless me!" (Gen. 32:26).

Let Christians beware, however, of their own motivations and attitudes in the midst of marital trouble. The constant temptation of faith is the sin of self-righteousness. How easy it is for a Christian spouse to believe himself or herself innocent over against a non-Christian mate! When we are trying hard to live forgiving and loving lives, we can easily delude ourselves into thinking we have achieved perfection, adopting self-justifying and even condescending attitudes toward our sinful, and properly infuriated, spouses. We need to remember the Biblical teaching that "none is righteous, no, not one"

(Rom. 3:10) and that therefore we all walk in acceptance only by the mercy of God in Christ. True faith should breed not pride, but repentance and humility, the acknowledgment that both we and our mates are totally dependent for our righteousness and relationship on the forgiveness and compassion of God.

Divorce is never the intention of God for our marriages. We can make such a general statement on the basis of the Biblical evidence. But there are some situations in which divorce seems inevitable as a last resort for the Christian. Jesus said that Mosaic law allowed divorce "because of your hardness of heart" (Mark 10:5 and pars.), that is, because human beings rebel against the will of God and refuse to follow it. Certainly we persist in such stubborn and sinful ways today. Christ could heal our marriages; there is no doubt about that. He has conquered our sin by his death and resurrection. Even the terrible perversions that warp our wedded ways could be made right and whole by his power, if we would but let him have his way with us. But we do not, and so our homes are haunted by chaos and hurt and conflict. Finally our devils drive us apart and make divorce seem the lesser evil. We subject our children to the shattering necessity of choosing between parents, while we ourselves limp off alone, bruised and bleeding, with broken hearts and psyches, perhaps pretending that such disruption of our lives is after all "for the best," when the truth is that we shall never again be quite whole and sane, unless God's healing is given.

Divorce is never "good," never "right," never "justified" in the eyes of God. Sometimes, on psychological grounds, we try to justify it as right, arguing that our children will be more deeply harmed if the marriage is continued, or stating, in religious terms, that the marriage allows no moral balance and must be terminated to allow us to be faithful. Let us stop kidding ourselves! Divorce is the result of our sin—the sin of us all—and we get ourselves into situations where it becomes inevitable, not by following the will of God, but by persistently refusing to do it. We reap what we sow, as Paul said (Gal. 6:7), and then increase the sin by having the gall to identify our action with the will of the righteous Father. It is like the game we Christians play with respect to war, if we want a parallel example. We know very well that we stand under that divine command, "You shall not kill" (Ex. 20:13), but we vote madmen into power, or allow racial and national hatred to fester, or create jobs by manufacturing tons of weaponry. Then when our sins of omission and commission mushroom to atomic bomb size, and the hatred of man for fellowman breaks out like a ravenous monster, we piously talk about "defending the right" and "peace with honor" and "just wars," and we rush out to slaughter hapless youths and civilians and identify it with the will of God.

The hypocrisy is obvious! Our sin can in no way be identified with good, and the sooner we take responsibility for it and stop trying to blame it on God, the sooner we may find healing. In the meantime, we need a sober reassessment of what we are doing in war, whether between nation and nation, or just between husband and wife.

Although neither divorce nor slaughter of our fellow human beings is ever good or right or justified in the eyes of God, our evil ways get us into situations where both seem necessary, where the only way to stop a Hitler, or to find any peace in a home, seems to be to declare a war, or to file a divorce suit in court. The attitude of the Christian who must enter into such evil but unavoidable solutions can only properly be one of deep anguish and repentance and realization that he or she is doing wrong, and his or her prayer can only be that nevertheless God will forgive.

For those who experience the agony of a broken home

with such an attitude, there is indeed forgiveness and acceptance and the opportunity of a new life, even in a new marriage, offered by the gospel. God tells us that he can make all things new (Rev. 21:5). Through the cross and resurrection of his Son, we can have a fresh beginning, if we cast ourselves on his mercy in true repentance for our wrong, and determine that in the future we will "turn around" and sincerely desire to do the right. Thus does Paul put it:

> If any one is in Christ, he is a new creation; the old has passed away, behold, the new has come. All this is from God, who through Christ reconciled us to himself and gave us the ministry of reconciliation; that is, God was in Christ reconciling the world to himself, not counting their trespasses against them, and entrusting to us the message of reconciliation. (II Cor. 5:17–19.)

The church, in its attitude toward divorced persons, should take special note of the last phrase in this quotation. We are entrusted with "the message of reconciliation." On the one hand, sincere and faithful persons who have found it necessary to divorce their mates sometimes have found themselves shunned and psychologically expelled by their fellow church members. It is as if somehow they had committed an unforgivable sin and were no longer worthy to attend a service of worship or congregational gathering. Such shunning is evidence of ignorance of the mercy of the very gospel church people profess, as if some sin could not be covered by the expiation of Jesus Christ! Similarly, such shunning is an incredible display of self-righteousness, as if another person's divorce were a more heinous sin than the church members' own pride or hatred! For those persons "who truly repent of their sins and who desire henceforth to live a godly and righteous life," the fellowship of the church must always be an open and receiving haven of love, of forgiveness, of understanding, of acceptance, and of mutual support.

On the other hand, some church members, including some members of the clergy, have adopted a "live and let live" attitude toward divorce. They have lightly concluded that the breakup of a home is a guiltless or even at times a proper procedure. Such clergy often perform marriage ceremonies for those who have glibly and willfully destroyed their former marriages, who carelessly assume that nevertheless they are acceptable to God, and who have no intention of mending any of their former ways. To such persons, the church must declare that God is not mocked, that those who divorce and remarry with such an attitude commit adultery in the sight of God (Mark 10:11–12). Their remarriage stands under the judgment of a Lord who will not take it lightly. God promises:

> Behold, I make all things new. . . . I am the Alpha and the Omega, the beginning and the end. To the thirsty I will give water without price from the fountain of the water of life. He who conquers [i.e., he who remains faithful] shall have this heritage, and I will be his God and he shall be my son. (Rev. 21:5–7.)

But then the passage continues:

> But as for the cowardly, the faithless, the polluted, as for murderers, fornicators, sorcerers, idolaters, and all liars, their lot shall be in the lake that burns with fire and brimstone, which is the second death. (Rev. 21:8.)

Our faithless age laughs at the imagery of such a Biblical quotation. We should remember that behind the imagery stands a very real God, who always holds us responsible for our actions.

CHAPTER 8

Knowing and
Being Known

Thou knowest me right well.
—Ps. 139:14

In Thornton Wilder's play, *Our Town*, the daughter, who has died in childbirth, is allowed to return to the land of the living for one day. In a poignant scene with her mother, she tries frantically to get the mother to take close notice of her, but her mother chatters on about the daughter's upcoming birthday party, about the presents, and other such everyday things. "Oh, mama," the daughter cries out in despair, "just look at me one minute as though you really saw me! . . . We don't have time to look at one another!"

It is a profound picture of our family life. We don't have time to look at one another. I wonder sometimes if our husbands suddenly were missing, whether we wives would be able to furnish a description of them. What was your husband wearing when he left the house this morning? Or where was he going when he left on that jet? Do you know exactly what his destination was, and where he would be staying? Sadly, many wives would have to plead lack of knowledge to those questions, just as husbands would be equally ignorant of their wives' doings and appearance.

We are the busiest and perhaps the loneliest people in
the world. From the time they enter school, our children
are overscheduled and undernoticed. We urge them into
music lessons, Scouts, Little League and sports, dancing
lessons, church groups, school activities, and hobbies,
and then we wonder why we do not know what they are
thinking.

As parents and mates, we hurry off in opposite direc-
tions, fathers to jobs, meetings, clubs, and sporting
events; mothers to P.T.A., volunteer groups, church circles, and bridge clubs, or to jobs, shopping, beauty shop,
and luncheons with the "girls."

As grandparents, we are isolated from the whirl, sent to
live in our retirement communities, with finally plenty of
time on our hands, but no one to share it with and few
meaningful pursuits. When someone dies and we go
through their effects and letters, we suddenly realize how
little we really knew them.

We have a vast and empty inner ache to know and be
known. We join yet another group to try to find some
meaningful relations. We go through encounter sessions,
where we pour out our hearts to strangers. We find
ourselves telling taxi drivers or bartenders all about our
families. Or we unload our hurts and anxieties on the
stranger or clergyman next to us on the plane.

It is this loneliness, this isolation from our loved ones,
which communication within a marriage can break
through and overcome. Indeed, if we are to know any
intimacy in this world, we must learn to know those we
hold dear and open ourselves to be known by them. "God
setteth the solitary in families" (Ps. 68:6, KJV) precisely
in order that we should be solitary no longer.

One of God's characteristics of which the Biblical
witness is sure, is that he, above all others, knows us
through and through. He knew us before we were born
(cf. Jer. 1:5; Ps. 139:15), and he knows our frame, because

he made it (Ps. 103:14). He knows the secrets of our hearts (Ps. 44:21) and the thoughts of our minds (Ps. 94:11). He knows our words before we speak them (Ps. 139:4) and the deeds we have done (Ps. 69:5). He knows our sufferings (cf. Ex. 3:7), and he knows us each by name (cf. Ex. 33:12, 17). We are told in the Gospel stories that Jesus too has such knowledge of us (cf. Luke 11:17). He knows what is in us (John 2:25), and he too knows our names (John 10:3), calling us and caring for us each individually. "I know my own and my own know me," he says (John 10:14).

Certainly we never can know one another as completely as our Lord knows us. Yet, because marriage is to be the imitation of Christ's love for his church, we are to know our mates with a knowledge approaching his. We too are to be able to say, "I know my own and my own know me."

It is this task of developing such communication and intimacy within our wedded unions which forms another of the major responsibilities of Christian marriage partners. By working at that task, by constantly striving to know and be known, in a lifelong process of communication, Christian partners deepen their intimacy and their commitment to each other and thereby live out their commitment to Jesus Christ. Such sense of intimacy brings with it some of the deepest satisfactions and joys of married life. Truly to know each other is never to be lonely again.

Unfortunately, when they enter marriage, many American couples start almost from scratch in learning to communicate. American courtship practices seldom encourage a young man and woman to know each other in depth before their wedding. The ideal of young love pictured in the television commercials is that of having "fun" together, of excitement, of openmouthed laughter. Couples rarely are presented with the thought that they should know each other in quiet moments, that they should share their backgrounds and values in serious conversation before they marry. There is no suggestion that they should see each other in their worst moments, as well as in their best—when they do not feel like smiling, or when their hair is dirty, or when they in fact have the flu; that they should know the person behind the toothpaste, the deodorant, and the cold remedies.

Perhaps one of the healthiest trends in American universities is that toward coed living, where young men and women learn to know one another in their dorms as people and friends in all the daily routines of their college life. There they see one another tousled before breakfast, tired from work, and washing their clothes in the laundry. They develop friendships and understandings of one another quite apart from the usual dating stereotypes. Anxious parents sometimes think that such coed living will lead to promiscuity and sometimes it does; but usually just the opposite is the case. Young people learn to know and appreciate one another as persons instead of merely as sexual objects and partners.

It has often been said that in order to be true lovers, married persons first of all need to be friends, and that is true. Any two people who intend to live with each other for the rest of their lives had better like each other and enjoy being together. Otherwise they are going to separate rather quickly after the honeymoon is over, or live together as perpetual strangers. Yet, even when we know another person as a friend, as well as a sweetheart before marriage, even when we have shared in depth during our courting, communication is a lifelong task which is never done at any period in the marital relation. People change and grow and mature, and it is constantly necessary to get to know the new persons that we become every day of our lives.

Some persons fear such intimacy in marriage. There is

a terrifying closeness about it, so that some persons fear if they are truly known, they will be rejected as unlovable or unworthy, or they will become too vulnerable to hurt or attack. All their lives, they try to hide behind a facade, or they resist forming any truly deep relationship. They end up living with their mates in name and address only, while really pursuing separate, private, and lonely lives.

One of the marvelous aspects of the Christian faith is that it is so realistic about what we are really like. Certainly the Biblical writers knew all about the glory and magnificence of human nature—our creative abilities, our capacities to love, our skill and courage and daring: "Nothing that they propose to do will now be impossible for them," acknowledges God at the Tower of Babel (Gen. 11:6). Our "beauty is like the flower of the field," says the writer of Isa., ch. 40 (v. 6). We do have our beautiful, tender, and lovely characteristics. But the Biblical writers also know all about our meanness, weakness, and violence; our petty sides, our scheming hearts, and frail and fleeting loyalties. We have only to read the book of Genesis, with its earthy portrayals of birth and death, of brotherly hatred, of jealousy and anger and envy, or the psalms with their laments and sufferings, their enemies and woes, and their sure knowledge that the span of our years is "but toil and trouble; they are soon gone, and we fly away" (Ps. 90:10). God knows what we are like, though we try to hide it from ourselves and our mates. "He himself knew what was in man," says The Gospel According to John of Jesus (John 2:25).

In the Biblical faith, there is never any illusion that you and I are saints, at least not according to the usual definition of the term.[72] When we share that faith, we therefore do not take with us into marriage unrealistic expectations about what we are like or are apt to do. We are, according to the Christian faith, a unique blend of saint and sinner, capable of the highest and most tender love and equally of the lowest spite and selfishness. Usually both sides of our natures are in full operation at any given time. We try to hide our sinful sides most of the time; the Christian knows that nevertheless his or her sin is there. In the last analysis, no one of us is fully lovable, and finally, we do not deserve the love that is freely given to us.

If we can acknowledge that in our marital unions, if we know we are both saint and sinner, if we realize that we live by the grace of love, rather than by earned merit and admiration, then we have the freedom to come out from behind our facades and to bare our souls, warts and all. That is, we have the freedom to be ourselves, *if we nevertheless are loved*. It is precisely the fact that such love is given in the Christian faith which makes such honesty possible. God knows us through and through. Jesus Christ knows what is in us. Nevertheless, God in Christ loves us and cares for us. We have the freedom, given by his love, to confess that we are sinners, openly and honestly to acknowledge the fact that we walk only by the grace of love. As the old evangelical hymn puts it:

> Just as I am, without one plea
> But that Thy blood was shed for me,
> And that Thou bidd'st me come to Thee,
> O Lamb of God, I come, I come!

It is the same freedom openly and honestly to be ourselves, to come out from behind our facades, to acknowledge that we are imperfect and weak and sinful —often selfish, often angry, often petty and careless— which is given us in the total commitment, which we have discussed, of Christian marriage. Partners to the committed marriage have no illusions about each other. They know they are always combinations of saint and sinner. Nevertheless they pledge to each other their lifelong and loyal love. On that basis, in the grace of love, they have the freedom to be themselves. They know they are accepted and cherished, each by the other, as they are, with nothing to hide. All the lines of communication open up for them.

Then how do we communicate with each other in Christian marriage? How can we come to know and be known?

Surprising as it may seem, one of the most important things any couple can do to communicate is to learn to practice trivia. It is enormously important in marriage, for example, that a spouse learns to greet his or her mate whenever he or she enters the room, even if the latter has only been gone a few minutes. It is important to notice the other's clothes and expression and walk, not necessarily commenting on them unless compliments are appropriate, but nevertheless consciously noting them in the mind. By doing such things, our spouses become "there" for us. We do not simply assume their presence nor do we settle down into the deadly routine of never looking at each other. It is amazing how many couples never really see each other—never note that the other has cut a finger, for example, or never see that the other looks fatigued. If we do not see each other, we really do not care.

I can recall the time in my childhood when my dad grew a mustache. For weeks, all of us in the family urged him to shave it off, because it made him look different and much older. Finally, he gave in, only to have no one notice for a week that he had done so. How frequently we don't have time to look at one another!

Similarly, couples need to practice in marriage the art of courtesy, the art of recognizing the presence and deeds of the other by the use of good manners. A simple "thank you" when the wife pours the coffee lets her know her husband sees her and appreciates her. A grateful comment, "How nice the yard looks," after the husband has mowed the grass, informs him that he is noticed and that his contribution is valued. Opening doors for each other, helping with carried bundles, holding tools, asking pardon for interruptions, inquiring how the other feels: these are the courtesies which we may extend to friends, but which are absolute necessities in the happy marriage. They say to the other person, "I see you, I appreciate you, I like you, I care about you." Many marriages that have not had them have ended in divorce on the ground of "indignities," for courtesy bestows on the one receiving it just that—dignity and worth. No relationship between human beings can long endure unless the participants are granted those qualities.

Communication—knowing and being known—demands perhaps above all else, sufficient time to take place. It took God two thousand years fully to reveal himself through the Biblical history. Surely we should expect it to take us at least a lifetime to make ourselves known to each other in marriage. We set apart special times to study and appropriate God's self-revelation. Equally we need special times every day to learn to know our marital partners. We cannot gain such knowledge if we are rushing from one activity to the next, and that certainly is at the root of the trouble with many marriages.

For one thing, family dining together seems to have become a lost custom. We have even built the habit of eat-and-run into our architecture: the snack counter, the bar stools, the TV trays—all have "hurry" or "do something else" built into their design. We never have time to loiter as a family over a meal. In fact, many families rarely eat together at all: each "cooks" his or her own breakfast before rushing off to school or work; lunches are grabbed on the run, or eaten in separate offices and schools; if dinner is eaten together, very often various members leave the table early, the children to rush off to

friends or homework, parents to watch the news, or go
to a meeting.

Mealtimes should offer an opportunity for families to
be together, to share their day's activities, to plan, or to
discuss some event. Politics, theology, race relations, job
problems, schoolwork, dates, vacations—the list of topics
that are aired around our family supper table is endless.
Before the circle is broken, we usually have managed to
share with one another just where we are and what it is
we think about the events that have taken place. Sometimes, after a lingering conversation, my husband will rise
to go watch the news on television, and our daughter will
say, "Daddy, stay a little while longer!" There is magic in
that sharing which binds a family together, and our
daughter is reluctant to end the sense of oneness that we
feel.

I shall never forget the woman whose husband was
transferred to another job and, after ten years of marriage, was able for the first time to eat his lunches at
home. The woman was terribly upset that her daily
routine was being interrupted! Her everyday life had
become so separate from her husband's that she could no
longer include him in it. So it is in many families, where
common meals are almost unknown. Such families sleep
under the same roof most nights, but they seldom have a
time when they really are conversing with one another.
Thus they fail really to know one another as the days and
years go by. In all our busyness, we may gain the whole
world, and lose our own souls at home, merely because
we never take the time really to find one another.

It is almost an American addiction to be doing something all the time. We feel guilty if we are just sitting
around talking, and not producing or learning. Even our
leisure time has become more and more like work. We
think we have to fill it by taking up a new hobby or by
producing a handcrafted object or by mastering a new

skill. We attend dozens of useless or dull meetings every year. We get ourselves into activities, because we feel "obligated." Our schedules are full from morning till night, our pace is frantic and fatiguing, and amid it all we are either too busy to spend time together or too tired to talk when we do get home. We are like a bunch of ants, rushing around, each efficiently doing his or her own job, and never uttering a word as we pass on our separate paths.

One pressure that contributes significantly to our pace is our terrible sense of "duty," our response to the almost continual urging by church or society, to "serve," to "help," to "support." We think we have to spend literally hours preparing a bazaar to raise money for some good cause, or we tramp through the neighborhood, collecting for one more charity. I do not want to underestimate the value of volunteer service; *some* of it does some good. But I shall never forget the juvenile court judge who, when asked by several clubwomen what they could do to combat delinquency, quickly and firmly replied, "Stay home." It was some of the best advice ever offered. There are hundreds of meetings held in church or school or civic clubs every year that do nothing but waste valuable time, which could so much better be spent at home with our spouses and children in conversation and sharing. As a member of the clergy and as a teacher for the church, I know that many church meetings should be bypassed, because they do society not half the good that our fellowship with our families would do. We need a firm sense of values, a sorting out of our priorities, to resist the "meeting pressures" on us. For too long the meetings have come first and our families have been ignored.

Husbands and wives must have time together regularly. That is a *sine qua non* of marriage, if a couple expect to share their thoughts and feelings in any meaningful way. Wise are the spouses who have built that time into their married routine. One couple I know have a "date" every Friday night. Sometimes they go out, sometimes they have friends in, sometimes they simply talk together or share television or read aloud; but that time is absolutely uninterruptible on their weekly calendars. Another couple make a practice of assessing their schedules every month or two. When the husband has had lots of business trips and they feel they are losing touch with each other, they call a halt to outside engagements and deliberately "catch up" on each other's doings, reviewing together all that has happened and how they feel about it. In another marriage, the husband enjoys having his back scratched every night as a release from the tensions of the day, and for twenty or thirty minutes before the couple go to sleep that ritual invariably takes place. The wife does not consider it a burdensome duty, because it always gives them time together. In fact, quarrels have to be patched up before bedtime, in order that the husband can get his scratching! It does not much matter how time together is gained. The important thing is that both husband and wife agree that gaining it is absolutely necessary.

Time together does not necessarily spell communication between a husband and wife of course. Some spouses have lots of time and do nothing but argue meaninglessly, others share an almost wordless and boring routine of sameness. For communication in marriage to take place, there must be, therefore, words spoken by means of which thoughts and feelings and inner lives are truly shared. It is significant that when God wanted to reveal himself to us, he spoke a word, and the word that was incarnate in Jesus Christ was the communication of God's actual and inner nature.

Some persons are afraid of words. They fear to share some information because of the response that it will elicit ("Honey, I just bashed in a fender on the car"). Or they withhold information in order to manipulate their spouse's behavior ("If I tell her I got a raise, she'll just rush out and spend it"). When such subterfuges take place, communication has broken down, and any marriage in which communication is lacking is a marriage headed for trouble. It is always amazing to read the advice columns in the newspaper and to see how often married couples could solve their problems if they would just tell each other what is on their minds. But for many reasons—and fear is the primary one—they will not speak their piece. Others do not communicate because they are not used to sharing feelings. Men especially somehow feel ashamed to talk about their emotions. Still others do not speak, because they have been too often interrupted, or because they have talked and talked and never really been heard.

There are dozens of programs springing up throughout the United States in which married couples are being taught, literally, to talk with each other. In one of these, called the Roman Catholic Marriage Encounter Movement, couples "10-and-10" every day. That is, sometime during the day—on the commuter train or after the kids have left for school—husband and wife separately sit down and write letters to each other for ten minutes "in loving detail," giving their feelings on such weighty topics as God, death, love, and sex, as well as on more mundane ones such as reaction to business trips. Later, when the couple are together, the letters are exchanged and at least ten minutes are given to each spouse to respond to what has been written. The result is new communication and understanding, learning about each other's feelings never before imagined possible, and deepened and newly appreciated relations between the mates involved.[73]

In other programs, mates are taught how truly to listen to their partners. They are required to be silent while the other expresses himself or herself, then they respond by restating what has been said, to make sure it has been understood correctly. Finally, they give their own response to their mate's words. By undergoing such discipline, mates learn—sometimes for the first time—really to hear what the other is saying and to interpret it correctly. It is a discipline that could easily be practiced in any home.

Not all couples need formal programs to open their lines of talking and listening. But in all marriages, partners need to be able to express their innermost thoughts and feelings openly and honestly, in the assurance that they will be listened to, understood, and gladly received, even when such openness brings up problems that must be resolved ("I really do not like the idea of your mother coming to spend a month with us this summer"), or expresses truths that are not pleasant ("You repeatedly interrupted me when I was trying to talk at the dinner party last night"). Problems, difficulties, irritations laid out in the open can, with mutual goodwill, be discussed and overcome. Kept hidden away, they sometimes multiply until they become completely unmanageable. In fact, one of the difficulties many couples have is that they never talk openly until a crisis arises; then sometimes it is an almost impossible task to sort out stored-up thoughts and emotions.

There is nothing more foolish and no habit more widely practiced in marriage than that of assuming we know what our mates think or feel, or that we know what their inner motivations and goals are ("Oh, I know what he would say if I told him about that"). By not plumbing each other's depths, by assuming we can read each other's minds, by presupposing we know what the other is like, we come to take each other for granted. When we do so we not only build up trouble for our marriages but we miss the marvelous inner life of the miracle—yes, miracle—which is our mate. There is nothing more "fearfully and wonderfully made" (Ps. 139:14, KJV) than the human personality. When you stop to think of it, each of us is a combination of our past home life, of the personality of our parents and dozens of others with whom we have come in contact, of accumulated learnings and traditions and values, all woven together in a unique way by our own unique gifts and genes. Moreover we are constantly changing and interacting under the influence of present persons and experiences. The resultant being, the consciousness that is "you" or "I" is a phenomenon found nowhere else on the face of the earth. What an opportunity to explore the depths of the totally new and different is given us in the opportunity to know each other in marriage! Just hearing the stories that come out of a mate's memory of his or her childhood can be a fascinating adventure in probing the unknown—and one, incidentally, that enthralls and delights our children. The more our daughter hears of her father's childhood, the more she wishes she could have known him as a boy, and the more I come to understand him as a man.

Let us, however, be realistic in this discussion of communication. Sharing feelings and thoughts and inner lives can be overdone. Some spouses seem to feel that they should wear their emotions on their sleeves, that every passing opinion and feeling should be dumped on their mates. Consequently their life together becomes a process of "navel-gazing," of dissecting every minute part of their inner lives, of concentrating endlessly on the working of their own psyches. I shall never forget the early days of my own marriage. Eager to know my husband intimately, I engaged in this process of introspection, often asking him what he was thinking, telling him how I felt, and asking his feelings on the subject. With infinite good sense, my husband called a halt to the introspection and pointed out that life could not successfully be lived if we were continually pulling out our psychological roots for the purpose of inspection. He was quite content to let us get to know each other gradually as we shared our daily routine and work together. In truth, so must it be. Communication in marriage really is not a process of concentrating on one's self, but of sharing and talking and discussing openly with one's mate, as one concentrates on living. We are called in the Christian faith, not to a life of self-examination, but to a life of service to the world. We exercise that service in our work, in our relations with our neighbors, in our worship and prayer, in our citizenship, in raising our kids and spending our money and solving our problems and planning our futures—in short, in all the many-faceted responsibilities of modern day-to-day living. The sharing of one's "everydayness"—that finally is the content of marital communication. It is all the problems, stresses, joys, and adventures of living a worthy life in the world.

The Biblical faith really is not mystically oriented, nor is it basically concerned with our inner selves. For example, one finds scenes in the Bible in which the life of self-examination and mystical contemplation would seem the natural outcome: Elijah on the mountain of God, hearing the still small voice (I Kings, ch. 19), the disciples on the Mount of Transfiguration, beholding the glory of the Christ (Mark 9:2–8 and pars.). But in both instances, the participants return quickly to the valley, Elijah to start a political revolution, the disciples to follow their Lord to Jerusalem and the cross. The personal religious experience, the communion with God, are given only for a purpose—to accomplish God's will among men on earth. There is no escape from the swirl and dust, the suffering and struggles of the life of ordinary mortals. We Christians are called to exercise our discipleship of marriage in the traffic of American society, not to retreat into isolated self-examination and sharing within our own four walls.

Similarly, the content of our sharing should be not merely our own inner experience, but that experience as it is engaged with the world in responsible service of God's will. For example, in those prophetic books, especially The Book of Jeremiah, where we are given some account of the prophet's inner life, we find that God never gives two hoots about the prophets' psyches in themselves. The prophets never are asked by the Lord if they are happy in their jobs, or how they feel about this or that divine command. "To all to whom I send you you shall go," Jeremiah is told in his call, "and whatever I command you you shall speak" (Jer. 1:7). When Jeremiah later starts complaining about the emotional and mental suffering that his prophetic office brings upon him, God tells him that he will succor him only as the prophet faithfully returns to his job (Jer. 15:15–21). We Christians have work to do; that really is the burden of the message. We are put on earth and given our beloved mates in order to do God's will. Communication in Christian marriage must not lose sight of that divine purpose, must not turn in upon itself, as if the creation of our own happiness were the sole reason for our lives together.

In some marriages, such as my own, husband and wife have the same profession. It is therefore very easy to share and to discuss our work together. In most marriages, the mates have different jobs, and it is not always easy to talk together about the tasks in which each is engaged. Tired husbands at night listen only halfheartedly to the wife's problems with the kids. Uninvolved wives find it difficult to comprehend the economics and tensions of a husband's business. Yet it must be realized that usually our work is the central focus of our lives, and if that cannot adequately be shared in marriage, we are not communicating that which occupies the most prominent positions in our thinking, feeling, and planning. Wives should not assume that they cannot understand what their husbands are doing at the office. Certainly they can grasp the basic facts of engineering or economics or sales and they then can comprehend what those things mean to their husbands. Husbands may not know how to bake a cake, or the latest theories of public education, but they can be an appreciative recipient of the first and a sounding board for the second. Openness to new learning, appreciation for others' different experience, eagerness to have one's own perspectives broadened, lend sincere interest and receptivity to our listening to our mates' accounts of their jobs. Above all, it deepens our admiration for and appreciation of our spouses. It is wonderful to know someone who can handle a job or a problem as capably as can my husband. When we tell our mates we feel that way, it does wonders for their self-esteem.

We must realize in our marital communication, furthermore, that we all need a life of privacy. Togetherness can be overdone. There are times when each spouse needs a space apart where he or she has the freedom and time to develop his or her own capabilities, the opportunity to be his or her own person. It is significant in the Old Testament that the root meaning of the Hebrew word, "to be saved," is "to be spacious," "to have room." When we are saved by God, in Old Testament terms, when we are whole persons, then we have room to live, we have space to spread out and be ourselves. In this sense, we all need that room, that space to spread out and develop our personhood.

Psychologists long have taught that every person must feel that he or she has some worthwhile talent or skill or achievement in order to have any sense of self-esteem. There must be something that each of us can excel at or achieve or master in order for us to have a feeling of self-worth. If we have no problems at all to overcome, we feel frustrated. If we have abilities that we never exercise, we feel unfulfilled and incomplete. The women's movement has capitalized continually on such feelings of "unfulfilled" women. There are many who are fed up with living only through their husbands' achievements and who have not been allowed to achieve anything as separate persons.

The point is that achievement in our own right takes time and space apart from our mates. It may be learning to cook or sew, playing the piano or painting, writing, gardening, working in the community, even visiting and developing friendships. Whatever our particular gift or skill, we must be able to feel we can do it on our own, and the wise mate allows the other the right to develop his or her own achievement. The wife who nags her husband for spending hours in his woodworking shop, the husband who berates his wife for her time spent visiting with the neighbors, may be digging at the very achievement from which that wife or husband gains her or his sense of self-worth. We must be wise enough to sense what it is that gives our partners a feeling of achievement, and then let them have the privacy and freedom to enjoy that activity.

Yet, let it be emphasized again that the development of our own individual personalities is not the goal, either of marriage or of the Christian way of life. That is what the women's movement has failed to realize, and it is the Achilles' heel of many modern self-help movements. Salvation has come to be equated with personal fulfill-ment, and transactional analysis or encounter groups, or women's liberation or "open marriage" is understood as the magic key to finding it. But woe to the person who sets out to fulfill only himself or herself! We were made to serve others and God, and in seeking only our own lives, we end up losing them instead. We must have room to live as achieving and whole persons, to be sure, but finally that achievement and wholeness must be placed in the service of another.

What point is there really in developing our own

personalities, unless they serve some higher purpose that lasts beyond our span? I think of my own parents, who were enormously gifted and talented individuals, who developed skills and intellectual abilities admired by many people. The skills lessened, the minds blurred, the gifts and talents faded, and finally they were at the end, feeble and forgetful old people. Is the human personality to be honed, only then to die and turn to dust? Or is it to be used in the service of a purpose that outlasts our waxing and waning, and that finally issues in an eternal kingdom on earth of love and joy and righteousness? If there be any meaning to human struggle and care, I must opt for the second view. Death makes a mockery of all our pretensions at ultimate self-worth and achievement.

Translated into practical terms of everyday married life, that means our privacy to develop our own person-hood has limits set upon it. We are not to be our own private persons to the detriment of our marriages. You may be skilled at making friends and it may give you great satisfaction, but your gift is also to be used to be a friend to your mate. Your spouse may be highly talented, respected by colleagues and critics, but those talents do not relieve him or her from responsibility for the family. I think of a scholar I once knew who shut himself in his study for eight hours a day and completely abandoned his responsibility for raising his children to his wife. He became highly respected in his field, but I Timothy has some harsh words to say to such people:

> If any one does not provide for his relatives, and especially for his own family, he has disowned the faith and is worse than an unbeliever. (I Tim. 5:8.)

We must be willing to be interrupted in our privacy and self-development. I may be banging furiously at the typewriter, but when my husband comes in with "It's time for a little something," it is time to stop and chat and have a cup of coffee together.

Above all, we must be willing to coordinate our own private goals with the priorities, schedules, and goals of our mates. For far too long, husbands have not given a second thought to uprooting their families if a promotion demands that they move to another city. Now unfortunately, far too many "liberated" women are not giving a second thought to the rights of their families as they scramble for recognition and honors. There is a thin line which must be walked between self-development and family good, and it takes the utmost in consideration and planning for a husband and wife to walk it. In my own marriage, my husband is often asked if I would be willing to speak or teach before some group. He invariably replies, "I don't know; ask her"—he unfailingly recognizes my independence as a person in my own right. Balancing that, I would not think of accepting a speaking engagement until I cleared the date with my husband and children and made sure that it was not going to disrupt important plans they had made. Personhood and family good must constantly be kept in balance. Neither privacy nor togetherness must take sole place in a family's life. Both must be guarded and cultivated in our communion with one another.

Capping the communication of husband and wife—the knowing and being known—is their life of physical and sexual intimacy together, and it is this means of communication with which we will deal in the next chapter.

CHAPTER 9

The Unique and Tender Knowledge

This is the will of God, your sanctification: that you abstain from immorality; that each one of you know how to take a wife for himself in holiness and honor, not in the passion of lust like heathen who do not know God; that no man transgress, and wrong his brother in this matter, because the Lord is an avenger in all these things, as we solemnly forewarned you. For God has not called us for uncleanness, but in holiness. Therefore whoever disregards this, disregards not man but God, who gives his Holy Spirit to you.

—I Thess. 4:3–8

How should we regard sex? If couples are confused about the answer to that question these days, there is ample reason. They are being barraged by a variety of views concerning sexual activity, its importance, its meaning, and its method.

If the marriage manuals are to be believed, then good sexual adjustment, frequent intercourse, and simultaneous orgasm on the part of both partners are the ideal goals of every marriage. If popular books are the guide, then bizarre methods and changing locales are the spice of sexual life. If clinical studies are what one reads, performance is all-important. By all of these, couples are given the idea that they should get in bed and achieve! The American view of achievement and performance as the basis of worth has been transferred to the bedroom.

On the other hand, the radical women liberationists are loudly proclaiming that sex as it has been practiced in American society is basically an evil, a tool of male power and manipulation used against dependent females to turn them into sexual objects and unthinking physical beings. Sex therefore in this view is to be avoided when it symbolizes male domination. Females are better off with masturbation or homosexual relations, although they too can seize the initiative and use their sex as a sign of their freedom.

Among our youth, sexual relations are often the natural and "friendly thing to do," a means of getting to know someone more intimately and personally. Sometimes it is a protest against the depersonalization and materialism of our bureaucratic society, but certainly a natural and necessary part of human relations.

In the daily newspaper, sex is an ugly and aggressive side of our society. It is the rising incidence of rape of women on our city streets, the horrible sexual torture and murder of adolescent hitchhikers, or the perverted motive of the kidnapper or of the child molester.

For some, sex is the X-rated movie showing at the local drive-in, the topless waitress serving drinks at the all-night bar, the massage parlor or the go-go girl or the porno film at the stag club.

Sex takes a multitude of forms in our multifaceted society. From all sides couples receive the stimuli of its differing definitions. Unless they wish to fall victim to our society's warped views of sex, unless, as Ephesians puts it, they wish to be "tossed to and fro and carried about with every wind of doctrine, by the cunning of men, by their craftiness in deceitful wiles" (Eph. 4:14), couples must have, in this area too, a sure foundation for their relationship. Once again the word of God forms the rock upon which we can firmly build.

That sounds immediately repressive and prudish to a lot of couples, and not without reason. If any institution has a bad record of teaching with regard to sex, it is the Christian church. For centuries, the church abandoned the Scriptures and considered the sexual urge as evil. One has only to read some of the statements of the early church fathers to find how negatively they treated the subject.[74] To be sure, they defended marriage and procreation as good, over against those heresies such as Gnosticism which regarded fleshly life as evil, but the passion connected with the sexual urge always made it suspect. To give only one example, Roland Bainton describes Augustine's position this way:

> Since procreation is definitely approved, the sexual act as such cannot be wrong. Nevertheless it is never without wrong accompaniments. There is never an exercise of sex without passion, and passion is wrong. If we could have children in any other way, we would refrain entirely from sex. Since we cannot, we indulge regretfully. Augustine almost voices the wish that the Creator had contrived some other device.[75]

At the same time that it frowned on the passion of sex, the earlier church also exalted celibacy as a higher state, a position still held by Roman Catholicism today. In Protestantism, on the other hand, while there were occasional rejections of the physical relationship in marriage, even the Puritans affirmed the goodness of the sexual relationship.[76]

Nevertheless, there is in Protestantism another movement that has had a subtle effect on our views of sex. Whether we are conscious of it or not, we tend to value things spiritual more highly than things physical. This is a legacy we have received from Pietism. I shall never forget the time when our daughter was in kindergarten. Shortly before Thanksgiving, the teacher asked the class what they should be thankful for, to which our daughter innocently replied, "Money." "Well," responded the teacher hesitantly, "I'm not sure we should be thankful for money." Money, politics, jobs, sex—these are all of the material world, having little to do with spirituality and holiness and the higher reaches of the soul. We never think of a "spiritual personality" as being at the same time a sexual creature—hence our shock over Mary Magdalene's love song to Jesus in *Jesus Christ Superstar.* Sex and religion, to our way of thinking, are incompatible opposites.

In short, Protestantism too shares to some extent the view that sex is sinful, if not downright "dirty." Protestants therefore often react to sexual expressions in our society with a good deal of prudery. The worst sinner in our eyes is often the one guilty of a sexual offense, and we point first to increasing promiscuity as the sign of growing immorality. Indeed, sex and sin are often synonymous in our minds. It does not bother us half so much that people are proud or selfish as it does that they have committed some sexual trespass.

Human sexuality can be viewed in such fashion only by abandoning the Biblical faith. As we pointed out before, sex is understood as a good gift of God in both creation stories. In the first, God makes both male and female in his image (Gen. 1:27); the sexual distinction is built into the structure of creation, and God pronounces it "very good" (Gen. 1:31). In the second creation story, the woman is made from the rib of the man—originally they were one—and after the creation of the woman they long to become one again. Some commentators have suggested that Adam's ecstatic cry in Gen. 2:23, "This at last is bone of my bones and flesh of my flesh," follows upon his sexual union with his wife. Whether the text is to be interpreted in such a fashion or not, it witnesses strongly to the fact that sexual desire and oneness are good gifts of God, given to human beings out of God's love for them. Thus the Old Testament celebrates sex and stands in wonder before its mystery:

> Three things are too wonderful for me;
>   four I do not understand:
> the way of an eagle in the sky,
>   the way of a serpent on a rock,
> the way of a ship on the high seas,
>   and the way of a man with a maiden.
>   (Prov. 30:18–19.)

One entire book in the Old Testament, Song of Songs, is made up of nothing but love poetry, and some of that contains the most explicit sexual imagery. For example:

> How graceful are your feet in sandals,
>   O queenly maiden!
> Your rounded thighs are like jewels,
>   the work of a master hand.
> Your navel is a rounded bowl
>   that never lacks mixed wine.
> Your belly is a heap of wheat,
>   encircled with lilies.
> Your two breasts are like two fawns,
>   twins of a gazelle.
>   (Song of Songs 7:1–3.)

In Gen. 18:12, Sarah speaks of sexual intercourse as "pleasure" (cf. Ezek. 16:37; Ps. 147:10), and the word comes from the same root as that used for "Eden" or "paradise." In the New Testament, I Tim. 4:1 ff. attacks those who counsel asceticism, "who forbid marriage and enjoin abstinence from foods" (I Tim. 4:3). The reasoning is that "everything created by God is good, and nothing is to be rejected if it is received with thanksgiving" (I Tim. 4:4). In both Ex. 21:10 and I Cor. 7:3 ff., sex is necessary to marriage, and husband or wife is not to deny the mate conjugal rights. There is nothing in the Bible that would condone the Victorian commandment to wives to indulge in intercourse, but never, never to enjoy it. The Biblical writers revel in the goodness of God's creation, and sing and shout out their praise to God for the way he has made it.

It must also be realized that in the Biblical faith, there is never any split made between the material and spiritual worlds. In fact, Christianity is one of the most materialistic religions known to man. Consider, for example, how often the message of the New Testament centers around eating.[77] Or think of the earthly rewards that are promised to those who are faithful (Mark 10:29–31 and pars.; Deut. 28:1–14), or the emphasis put on the physical nature of the resurrection (Luke 24:36–43; John 20:24 to 21:14). Or consider that in the Kingdom of God, there will be eating and drinking (Mark 14:25 and par.; cf. Matt. 22:1–14 and par.). Think of all those times when Jesus healed not only souls but bodies. The stuff of the physical world is very much of concern to God, and while Jesus does not wish us to put our trust in material things, he is concerned with our material welfare and promises physical as well as spiritual wholeness (cf. Rev. 21:3–4). His healings, for example, are the firstfruits of life in the Kingdom of God.

In the Biblical view, human beings are always considered as psychophysical wholes. They cannot be split into separate parts of soul and body, mind and spirit. They are always one, with the whole person engaged in any act. When the psalmist hungers after fellowship with God, it is with his flesh as well as his spirit:

> O God, thou art my God, I seek thee,
>   my soul thirsts for thee;
> my flesh faints for thee,
>   as in a dry and weary land where no
>   water is.
>
>   (Ps. 63:1.)

The psalmist's flesh cries out in praise to God:

> How lovely is thy dwelling place,
> O LORD of hosts!
> My soul longs, yea, faints
> for the courts of the LORD;
> my heart and flesh sing for joy
> to the living God.
> (Ps. 84:1–2.)

This flesh trembles before the awesome presence of the Lord:

> My flesh trembles for fear of thee,
> and I am afraid of thy judgments.
> (Ps. 119:120.)

As these quotations show, a person's flesh is understood in The Psalms as one and synonymous with a person's being, and to talk about a person's spiritual relationship to God is at the same time to talk of that person's body. Deutero-Isaiah can therefore say that in the last days, all flesh will see the glory of the Lord (Isa. 40:5), all flesh will know that the Mighty One of Jacob is Savior and Redeemer (Isa. 49:26), all flesh shall come to worship before the Lord of Israel (Isa. 66:23). In such passages, "flesh" is synonymous with "person."

For this reason, the New Testament never speaks of the immortality of the soul, but only of that resurrection of the body in which the whole person is included. It knows nothing of a spiritualized Jesus, condemning all who would deny that the Son of God really lived life fully in the flesh (I John 4:2; II John 7). To speak of human beings in Biblical terms means to include the body, and when Paul opposes the life in the flesh to life in the Spirit, for example, in Rom., ch. 8, or Gal. 5:16–26, he is speaking not of separate parts of a person but of human beings redeemed or unredeemed. For Paul, too, human beings are one, and they are related to God not only in their spirit but also in their bodies, which are understood as an essential part of their being (Rom. 8:23; I Cor. 6:12–20). "Glorify God in your body," writes Paul (I Cor. 6:20), because it is the temple of the Holy Spirit. Human beings, to be understood in the context of the Biblical faith, must be seen as psychophysical wholes.

This means that the life of sex can never be separated, for the Christian, from the life of spirituality. It is fully as possible to violate or to fulfill our relation to God through sexual activity as through prayer or service. We are involved in what we do with our bodies and cannot separate our selves from their activities.

This is one of the reasons why the Biblical witness stands opposed to all "casual" views of sex. Premarital intercourse, or fornication, is uncompromisingly opposed (Ex. 22:16–17; Matt. 15:19; Acts 15:20, 29; 21:25; I Cor. 6:15–20; I Thess. 4:3–4), because it is an attempt to engage in sexual activity apart from the total commitment of the self in marriage, and that is a perversion of God's intention for us. In ancient Israel, the woman who engaged in premarital relations was stoned to death (Deut. 22:20–21), while a man was forced to marry any virgin whom he violated (Deut. 22:28–29). Today, such laws would pretty well decimate the population. But the point is that the Biblical writers will settle for nothing less than the involvement of the whole self in the sexual act. Thus, Israel also forbade bestiality (Lev. 18:23; 20:15–16; Deut. 27:21), that perverted act which would satisfy sex only as a biological urge and which would thereby turn a human being into an animal. We are not to use our bodies in a manner that would deny our spirit.

Indeed, Paul says that it is actually impossible to do so. We are always involved in every act we do with our bodies, and if we pervert the God-given function of our bodies, we pervert also our souls: "Do you not know that he who joins himself to a prostitute becomes one body with her? For, as it is written, 'The two shall become one.' . . . The immoral man sins against his own body. Do you not know that your body is a temple of the Holy Spirit within you, which you have from God?" (I Cor. 6:16, 18–19). Paul is arguing here that we may think we can indulge in sexual intercourse with no commitment of our inner selves, but actually our total self is involved and will be perverted by our immoral act. The truth of Paul's insight is perhaps evidenced by the fact that the result of illicit relations is often disgust, repulsion, even hatred of self, because the self has been so cheaply valued and used. It is also the case that premarital sexual relations often have a negative effect on subsequent marital relations, resulting in guilt or frigidity or other personality disturbances.

God does not intend us to descend to the level of animals, nor does he wish us to join bodies without joining lives. Karl Barth has put it this way:

> Coetus without co-existence is demonic. What are you, you man and woman who are about to enter into sexual relations? What do you really want of each other? What is your business with each other? What do you have in common? Is there any meaning in it? Is it demanded and sustained by your real life together? . . . This is the challenge of God's command in relation to this particular human activity.[78]

On the basis of such arguments, however, some theologians have maintained that premarital or extramarital sexual relations are not improper if they truly involve the commitment of the self. The title of "the New Morality" has been given to such views, and they are represented by Harvey Cox in his earlier book, *The Secular City*:

> By definition, premarital refers to people who plan to marry someone someday. Premarital sexual conduct should therefore serve to strengthen the chance of sexual success and

fidelity in marriage, and we must face the real question of whether avoidance of intercourse beforehand is always the best preparation.[79]

Bishop J. A. T. Robinson concurs:

> The decisive thing in the moral judgment is not the line itself [between marital or extramarital sex] but the presence or absence of love at the deepest level.[80]

Such views really leave couples standing on quicksand. They assume that a man and woman, inflamed by sexual desire, can judge whether or not love is present "at the deepest level," or whether or not premarital intercourse will better prepare them for marriage, or indeed, whether or not they are committed to each other at all. With our human propensity to rationalize in order to gain our own selfish ends, it is doubtful that couples in such a situation can make such judgment accurately. It can certainly be said, as we stated in Chapter 3, that couples before marriage have not really committed themselves to each other fully because they have not in fact acted out that commitment. They have not left father and mother behind and cleaved to each other alone. They have not taken on the responsibility of housing and clothing and feeding each other, of bearing each other's burdens and faults and of answering to society for each other. They have not become primarily responsible for the welfare and happiness of another human being, and they have not committed themselves irrevocably to a relationship that they cannot at some future point abandon. To enter into sexual relations with such a lack of commitment is therefore to pervert oneself, to misuse one's spirit by the misuse of one's body, to violate the intention God has for the relation of male and female.

If we ask just exactly what God's intention is for us in sexual activity, certainly we have to answer that procreation is one of his purposes (Gen. 1:28). Yet, in the Biblical witness, that is not God's primary purpose. The primary purpose of sex according to Genesis, and to Jesus, who quotes Genesis, is to unite two people: "The two shall become one. So they are no longer two but one. What therefore God has joined together, let not man put asunder" (Mark 10:8–9; Gen. 2:24). The function of sex is a unitive function. Sex is to be a "knowing," a way of intimacy that can be realized in no other way. Just as we know God in a unique way through the Sacraments, so also we know each other in a unique way through sexual intimacy.

At its best, sexual intercourse is a kind of flowing together: an overwhelming hunger and drive to join bodies as one, a feverish working together for realization, ecstasy so great it is almost painful, and then release, deep contentment and security and happiness in the arms of each other. In the process of sexual intercourse, we feel as if the most hidden inner depths of our beings are brought to the surface and revealed and offered to each other as the most intimate expression of our love. All we are as male or female becomes open to the other, and is made complete by being joined with the inner self of one's mate. We know each other and become one with the other and are fulfilled by each other in a way otherwise utterly impossible, and that knowing and that fulfillment carry over into our whole married life, and strengthen and deepen and periodically refresh it.

The Biblical writers witness to this unitive function of sex by the very vocabulary they use. Throughout the Old Testament, sexual intercourse is described as a "knowing": "Adam knew Eve his wife" (Gen. 4:1) or "Elkanah knew Hannah his wife . . . ; and in due time Hannah conceived and bore a son" (I Sam. 1:19–20). Indeed, this vocabulary is carried over into the language about God, and the intimacy of God's relation with his people is expressed by this "knowing":

> I am the LORD your God
>   from the land of Egypt;
> you know no God but me,
>   and besides me there is no savior.
> It was I who knew you in the wilderness,
>   in the land of drought.
>   (Hos. 13:4–5.)

In order to express the promise that he will redeem his people Israel in the future, God uses the metaphor of marriage: "I will betroth you to me in faithfulness; and you shall *know* the LORD" (Hos. 2:20, italics added). When Israel becomes a faithless adulterer toward her divine husband, it is said that then there is "no *knowledge* of God in the land" (Hos. 4:1, italics added).

We must be clear about how the Old Testament intends this sexual language, however. When it is used of God it is only metaphorical, and there is never any thought in the Bible that sexual intercourse can be revelatory of God, a fact that many contemporary writers on marriage have failed to realize, but a fact that is important for our understanding of sex. The reason for this, moreover, is very clear: Israel was surrounded on every side in the ancient Near East by peoples who practiced fertility rites in their religion. It was thought in those pagan religions, just as it is thought in many religions today, that the life of nature and of man were one, and that by the exercise of cultic prostitution, the fertility of nature could be magically coerced. Human fertility affected the fertility of the gods of nature. Through sex, it was thought, humans participated in the life of the divine. This thought is emphatically rejected by the Old Testament writers (cf. Hos. 2:2–13; Amos 2:7–8; Jer. 2:20–22; 2:23–28; 3:1–5; many other references). There is nothing of God revealed in the sexual act, and knowledge of him is not communicated in the mystery of sex. There is no doubt that the sexual life of human beings has a wonder and mystery about it, and the Biblical writers acknowledge this mystery, as we have said. They also warn us against calling that mystery "God," just as they warn us against giving God's name to anything in all creation (Ex. 20:4–6; Deut. 5:8–10). The teen-agers who think they have discovered something "divine" and beautiful in the backseat of an auto are not only kidding themselves; they are breaking God's commandments and blaspheming his holy name.

Sexual intercourse in marriage does bring with it knowledge of our mates and of ourselves, however, and that knowledge is such a profound communication and touches so deeply the center of our selfhood that it can be given in no other way. It is this which makes nonsensical so much of the sex education offered to our young people. We think we are going to teach them, openly and fully, about sex, and to be sure, the physiology, psychology, and theology of sex should be taught to them. But we delude ourselves if we think we have thereby exhausted the subject and prepared our young people fully. Try as we will, we cannot communicate the knowledge that is given in sexual intercourse.

This is one reason so many parents have difficulty talking about the sexual life with their children. They cannot express that which they have known, and in fact that knowledge is inexpressible outside of the situation. Yet, without the knowledge and communication that are given in sex, it seems like a bestial and abhorrent thing to many of our children. When confronted with the mechanics of sex, they often cannot believe that their parents would do such a thing. Sometimes they break into tears. And we parents are left stammering and stuttering in embarrassed confusion.

Perhaps the only way children can be taught about sex, having once been given the basic facts, is to see that their parents have a joyful and good conscience toward the subject. Then the children can believe that sex is good and that it is a mystery known only to married adults, who hold it in trust for them until they themselves marry and enter into it. Sex can only be presented to children fully as a promise to believe, because it involves a knowledge and communication of the self which children cannot possibly grasp.[81]

Because the sexual life of man and wife does involve this knowing, this communication of the self at its deepest levels, this also means that sex cannot be separated from the rest of married life. It is bound up with everything that husband and wife do in relation to each other. When sexual difficulties enter a marriage, they are very often symptoms of a deeper disturbance of the relationship. It must be emphasized, however, that this is not always true. There are some couples who simply lack essential sexual knowledge, or who suffer from specific fears or inhibitions and guilt as a result of childhood training or earlier experience. Just the common factors of fatigue and lack of time play an enormous role in sexual adjustment. Nevertheless, if a marriage is disturbed on other levels, new sexual techniques alone rarely will help it. Far too much emphasis has been placed on techniques and performance by popular articles and books. The sexual relation is only one part of the total marital relation. It alone can never carry or preserve the relationship, although it can certainly help. It is a tool that is given for the purpose of expressing the total relationship between man and wife, but it does express the relationship in a marvelous and joyful way, which adds to the intimacy and appreciation of a husband and wife for each other.

Sexual relations do not always have to be ecstatic and profound, of course. Sometimes they may be comfortably humdrum, or enchantingly playful. Patting, snuggling, touching, also deepen marital intimacy, and certainly are a pleasurable method of communication. Nevertheless they seem to mean most and are most satisfying, when the couple also are able at other times to enter into the ecstasy of orgasm. There is no substitute for the intimacy of that form of knowledge.

Because sexual intercourse is a means of communication at the deepest level, it is almost axiomatic that a couple cannot achieve their most satisfying sexual life together overnight. Sexual satisfaction, as with other forms of communication in marriage, is a gradual achievement, a process in which the couple learn and grow together in their appreciation and understanding of each other over the years. As in other areas, words are important here too—the frank and open discussion of each other's needs, of what is pleasant sexually and what is not, of any fears or problems that seem to interfere.

There is no marriage manual that can or should lay down rules for everyone. Every couple is different. Every individual has different needs, with respect to frequency, manner, and method of sexual activity. For example, some marriage manuals have held up simultaneous orgasm as the ideal for every couple, but it is perfectly possible to enjoy a satisfying sex life and never to have experienced such simultaneity. A wife may find that she needs the release of orgasm only occasionally and yet may thoroughly enjoy simply furnishing pleasure to her husband in between times. In sex, as in every other area of life, "the written code kills, but the Spirit gives life" (II Cor. 3:6). It is the heart, the love, the spirit of caring expressed by sex that is the most important. Trying to follow someone else's rules can turn the caring into an exercise in frustration. Sexual life, as all life, is given us as a good and merciful gift of God. He gives it to us that we may have joy—joy in the vitality that surges in us, joy in the closeness of the relationship with our mate, joy in the marvelous mystery that makes the two of us one, and binds us together in a unique and tender knowledge.

When a couple achieve such joy in such intimacy together, when through their years of living and working, of laughing and weeping, of celebrating and worrying together, they achieve that oneness of flesh that turns their marriage bed into a haven of security and tenderness and comfort, then they come to realize that God has indeed provided marvelously for them in marriage. They recoil in horror at the thought of ever spoiling that provision by breaking their covenant of faithfulness with each other. Inconstancy in the exercise of such a gift would be as horrible as if Christ were to say to his church, "I no longer faithfully love you; I am rejecting you and giving my love to another." That Christ would ever prove untrue is simply unthinkable. Equally unthinkable therefore should be the unfaithfulness of Christian mates, for Christ's love is the pattern of what our love for each other should be in marriage.

Unfortunately there are those who misuse and abuse God's good gift of sexuality. Rather than enjoying sex as a unique and tender means of loving communication, they employ it as an instrument of pride or power or aggression. We are all aware that some men use their sexual prowess as a tool of conquest. Whether we speak of the college man, sowing his wild oats among the local high school girls, or of the middle-aged man who sets out to prove that he is still sexually desirable to his secretary, we know that sex can be employed as a tool of power. There is no consideration in such a use of sex for the good of the other, much less of communication and lasting intimacy with her. She is being viewed simply as one to be conquered, like a trophy of war to be later exhibited and bragged over.

Females too are not exempt from the use of sex as a tool of power, for many are the women who employ their sexuality to manipulate a male. This is a use of sex that is widely advocated in American advertising, and women are urged every day to make themselves glamorous in order to control their men. ("Use Maybelline—for eyes a man can get lost in," or "Gentlemen prefer Hanes.") The women who seek such control give love or withhold it, in reward or punishment of their captive mates. Sometimes the marriage bed is turned into a battlefield, or the wife becomes a bait that always must be caught. As ludicrous as such games appear, they are widely practiced in the American home, and many are the subtle methods women use to set them up.

In any misuse of sex, it is obvious that the mate is considered little more than a thing. Certainly this is the case also where sex is pursued purely for selfish animal pleasure, where the physiological release afforded by orgasm becomes the all-important goal of one partner, apart from all consideration and concern for the needs of the other. Such selfish pursuit is little more than rape, and breeds in the partner so being used a feeling of disgust and repulsion.

Sometimes, in extramarital relations, sex is employed as a means of social approval, or even as a way of overcoming boredom. Similarly, sex can be an aggressive tool for wreaking vengeance on a lover or spouse or relative. ("If he's going to play around, then I'll show him two can play at this game.")

Perhaps we should also say a word about the perversion of God's gift of sex in homosexual relationships. Homosexuality has been loudly touted by radical members of women's liberation groups as a substitute for heterosexuality, and apparently it is freely practiced, not only within gay groups, but also in youth communes of various types. Certainly there is more acceptance of it in our society today than at any other time in our history. Some psychotherapists no longer consider it to be an illness, but simply a form of sexual behavior at variance with the norm. Homosexuality can assume as many forms as heterosexual relations and may be practiced for many differing motives. There is little doubt that some mature homosexual couples enjoy an intimate and loving relationship, in a lasting commitment to each other resembling heterosexual marriage. On the other hand, adolescent homosexual relations are usually of temporary duration, and within the women's movement, some homosexual relations are pursued purely for selfish physical pleasure.

Whatever the type of homosexual relationship involved, it is sheer fantasy to think that it can be an adequate substitute for the heterosexual relationship of a happy marriage. When a husband and wife know each other sexually, it is precisely their sexual difference which is communicated, both to themselves and to each other. They learn deeply what it means to be male and female, apart and together. The way male and female know each other is far different from the way male and male, or female and female, know each other. This is one of the stumbling blocks of the "sisterhood" of women's liberation. The "sisters" form close relationships, and the women may get along beautifully with each other. But they have not thereby developed that further communication of getting along with males or of entering into the most intimate relationship with the opposite sex, in the one-to-one intimacy of marriage.

For this reason, homosexuality, no matter how loving its nature (and far too often it is not loving at all, but a psychological aberration spawned by previous distorted relationships with parents in the home), must always be viewed as an aberration and often as a perversion of God's gift of sexuality. Certainly Paul understands it as an unnatural perversion (Rom. 1:26–27), and while we may not be as condemnatory as he, we should understand homosexuality as a use of sex not intended by God and therefore not finally to be encouraged or glibly accepted.

One of the tragic aspects of modern gay groups is that they often lock young persons into lifelong homosexual behavior, when those persons might grow and change and eventually achieve the true intimacy and joy of a happy and heterosexual marriage.

The methods of misusing God's good gift of sex are almost numberless, but as someone has wisely said, the best way of guarding against the abuse of sex is to put it to its proper use.[82] That takes time, it takes words, it takes consideration and concern for one's mate. Above all it takes the love that cherishes and honors for a lifetime. Only those who responsibly use God's gifts inherit the joy that comes from them, but oh, how tender and unique is the knowledge that mates have of each other in their unity of one flesh!

CHAPTER 10

Saying "Peace, Peace"

Woe to you, scribes and Pharisees, hypocrites! for you are like whitewashed tombs, which outwardly appear beautiful, but within they are full of dead men's bones and all uncleanness. So you also outwardly appear righteous to men, but within you are full of hypocrisy and iniquity.—Matt. 23:27–28

I know a fine Christian woman who has driven her husband to drink. She is loving, forgiving, irenic, and patient, and she simply drives her husband nuts, *because she will not listen seriously to him when he becomes angry.* For this woman, anger and conflict are wrong. Therefore when her husband shouts or rages, she waits out his anger patiently, and then tenderly forgives and forgets everything he has said. The result is that her husband feels he is beating himself against a stone wall. He cannot communicate his feelings to her, and so rather than engage in further frustration, he drowns his rage in a sea of alcohol.

Such couples, unfortunately, are the victims of Christian stereotypes. For many churchgoing couples, faith is incompatible with anger, and any conflict between persons is understood as a manifestation of sin. These are the couples who have been taught to believe that those smiling, well-scrubbed families pictured on the front of church publications represent the ideal in Christian family relations. For them, faith issues in perfect peace, undisturbed by any harsh words.

Actually, some conflict is inevitable in every marriage, Christian or not. No two persons want exactly the same things or see the world in exactly the same way, and the more intimate the marriage is, the more conflicting desires and views are likely to come to the surface. Further, there is nothing wrong with conflict, provided it is used constructively, as a means of communication, of understanding, and of strengthening and deepening the ties of intimacy.

The Biblical authors had harsh things to say about those who tried to pretend everything was all right rather than face honestly the faults in themselves and in their society. In the quotation with which we began this chapter, our Lord called such people "hypocrites," and in the following quotations from Jeremiah and Ezekiel, those two prophets sternly condemn the false prophets who were saying that all was well within Israel, when the quality of her life was totally at variance with the will of God.

> They have healed the wound of my people lightly,
>   saying, "Peace, peace,"
>   when there is no peace.
>
> (Jer. 6:14; 8:11.)

Because, yea, because they have misled my people, saying, "Peace," when there is no peace; and because, when the people build a wall, these prophets daub it with whitewash [cf. the wife above]; say to those who daub it with whitewash that it shall fall! There will be a deluge of rain, great hailstones will fall, and a stormy wind break out. . . . And I will break down the wall that you have daubed with whitewash, and bring it down to the ground, so that its foundation will be laid bare; when it falls, you shall perish in the midst of it; and you shall know that I am the LORD. Thus I will spend my wrath upon the wall, and upon those who have daubed it with whitewash; and I will say to you, The wall is no more, nor those who daubed it, the prophets of Israel who prophesied concerning Jerusalem and saw visions of peace for her, when there was no peace, says the Lord GOD. (Ezek. 13:10–11, 14–16.)

In the witness of the Bible, God is against any blind or "loving" phony acceptance of the *status quo*. When there is something wrong within an individual or a relationship or a society, God ferrets out the wrong and exposes it, sometimes quite violently. Then the wrong has the possibility of being healed and made right again. One is reminded of Jesus crashing into the Temple with that whip, overturning the tables of the money changers and condemning the people for thinking that they could hide their faults in the temple by turning it into a "den [i.e., hiding place] of robbers" (Mark 11:15–19). God wants the truth to come to light, and sometimes he himself engages in conflict in order to expose it.

So too is it with conflict and anger in marriage. They can be instruments of exposing the truth, of opening communication, so that the marital relationship may be healed and strengthened and made more intimate still. If, however, differences are buried in a marriage and a phony peace is preserved by one partner always giving in, then no honest communication is taking place. Silent, smoldering resentments are very likely present which may finally break out and destroy the home, or at least cost the silent partner his or her psychic health. Peace at any price—peace, peace, when there really is no peace—is not the equivalent of a happy marriage; rather it is a destructive denial of that truth necessary for a truly Christian marriage.

Many couples will not face the truth in their marriages. Some of them are too lazy to do so, preferring the simulated peace of noncommunication to the strenuous effort and occasional pain it takes to share their feelings with one another. Others assume that they know all there is to know about their partners, that they can read the other "like a book," or that their partner certainly ought to know how they feel. Some, like Edith Bunker, in *All in the Family* regard their marriage, while certainly less than ideal, about as good as it can be. Said Edith, "Well, my marriage works, and my father always used to say, 'When something works, don't fix it.'" Thousands watching the television show identified with Edith, because that is exactly the approach they take to their own imperfect relationships. But in real life, such resigned acceptance has led to countless mediocre marriages, in which, as the years progress, the couples feel their relationships become less and less satisfactory. In many such unions, the couples deny all differences until finally a serious crisis arises and then, usually too late, they show up at the door of the clergyman or the marriage counselor, with years of unresolved differences and buried resentments on their hands.

Another major task that the Christian couple face, therefore, in their effort to live out their commitment to each other and to Christ is the task of exposing and conquering their conflicts with each other. Only if, through the years, differences can be honestly faced and resolved, can a Christian couple deepen and grow in their marital commitment. It is this ability to solve differences together which separates highly successful marriages from the mediocre ones, and truly Christian marriages are not those in which there is only peace, but those in which there is honest communication and intimacy. Perhaps the church bulletin should carry on its cover sometime a picture of a mate *listening intently* as his or her partner talks angrily; probably it would be nearer to God's desire for us.

We have, throughout this book, taken the pattern for

Christian marriage from God's relation to his people, from Christ's relation to his church, as that is revealed to us through the witness of the Scriptures. That relation can also form the pattern for dealing with our conflicts in marriage.

The Lord is frequently angry with us; there is no doubt about that. We stand continually under his judgment, because of the wrong we do, and God brings the consequences of our sinful acts upon us. We suffer warfare, violence, aggression, pain, anxiety, and loss, because persistently we try to run our lives apart from the will of God. Yet, for all his anger toward us—and let no one think that God merely winks at our sin—God's judgment is characterized by three magnificent mercies.

First, it is always carried out for the purpose of recreating and restoring us to a proper relationship with himself. God's judgment is never merely vengeful or punitive, but rather is always redemptive. It is intended finally to purify us of our sin and to make us whole again (cf. Isa. 1:24–26; Zeph. 3:8–13; Hos. 3:1–5).

Second, God's judgment is always rendered in the context of his love and commitment. It is precisely because he loves us that he brings his wrath upon us (cf. Amos 3:2), and it is precisely because he has committed himself to be our God that we know his anger is not his last word toward us (cf. Isa. 51:1–3; Jer. 31:20; Hos. 11:8–9).

Third, God's judgment finally always carries after it the announcement of forgiveness, which makes possible the renewal of the relationship (cf. Isa. 54:4–8; Jer. 31:31–34; Hos. 14:4–8).

It is all three of these gracious mercies which are made flesh in Jesus Christ: he comes into the world bringing God's judgment on our sin (John 3:18 f.), yet his purpose is finally "not to condemn the world, but that the world might be saved through him" (John 3:17). So he brings

God's forgiveness to pass through the sacrifice of himself on the cross, and gives us the possibility of reconciliation and joy with the Father.

This pattern of divine mercy in God's argument with us can be most instructive for our marriages, for it can give the measure of what is constructive and destructive conflict. Before a couple decide to level with each other, to open up and reveal their anger, and expose their differences to each other, they need to judge whether their conflict will serve the purpose of improving their relationship. It is likely to be healthy or destructive?

Obviously a great deal of conflict and argument that occurs in marriage has no beneficial intent whatsoever. Some mates attack the other simply because they want vengeance on their partner; they want to wound and diminish their mate. They engage in name-calling, ridicule, and belittling practices that can be especially cruel when carried on in public ("Do you know my husband? He's the fat one over there"). They lay derogatory stereotypes on each other ("What a stupid thing to say; it's just like a woman to be so irrational"). Or they engage in the infuriating practice of amateur character analysis ("You always think you're so great; well, I happen to know you're compensating for an inferiority complex"). In such attacks, the purpose certainly is not to improve the relationship, but rather to triumph over the other, to hurt, to inflict wound for wound. Obviously such destructive conflict simply widens the gap between the partners. God in Christ engages in conflict with us for the purpose of improving our relationship with him. Couples need to remember that in their marital arguments.

When one partner has a gripe, when an argument is brewing, the questions to ask are these: Is this really something worth arguing about? Is this a persistent source of irritation in our relationship and therefore

something that must be solved, or am I only being petty
and picayune or perhaps even vengeful? Is this a fault in
my partner, or is it really in me or in someone else? Is
solving this problem worth the price of the argument we
will go through? How will my partner react, and what
changes can really be made? Will the solution of this
problem actually improve our relations with each other?
Psychotherapist George R. Bach has worked with thousands of couples' marital conflicts and has pioneered in
developing the concept of "fighting fair" in marriage. In
his book, *The Intimate Enemy: How to Fight Fair in Love
and Marriage*,[83] he has pointed out that in constructive
marital conflict both partners win the argument. That is,
the relationship is improved and therefore both benefit
from the fight.

This means, in the second place, that the couple must
be committed irrevocably to the relationship, and that
their argument must be carried out in the context of that
loving commitment as God's argument with us always is.
No marriage can long endure without the determination
to preserve it, come what may. Only the couple who
know that they both hold their union more important
than anything else can risk being fully open and honest
with each other in solving their differences. If there is the
fear that the disclosure of some significant difference may
destroy the union, open communication obviously will not
take place and real intimacy therefore will not be
achieved. One of the reasons we are able to tell God
everything in our prayers is that we know his love for us
persists, despite all our shortcomings. So too must it be
in our differences with each other in marriage.

When a couple value their relationship more highly
than the issues that divide them, they will not descend in
their arguments to quarreling over things that cannot be
changed. There are lots of differences in marriage that
can be overcome by mutual adjustment, growth, and

understanding, and above all, by a sense of humor. Human beings can change!—that is the presupposition of the Christian faith. There are also personality and family characteristics that cannot be changed, and there is no point in arguing about them ("I hate your thick ankles. Why couldn't you have inherited your father's legs?"). Reinhold Niebuhr's well-known prayer would be appropriate for couples:

> O God, give us serenity to accept what cannot be changed, courage to change what should be changed, and wisdom to distinguish the one from the other.

Couples who value their relationship more highly than their differences also will not engage in "dirty fighting" (Bach) or hitting below the belt. Everyone has vulnerable spots, those things about which he or she is especially sensitive. It may be a physical characteristic such as obesity or baldness, it may be a problem such as stuttering or shyness, it may have to do with one's self-image on the job or in the family. Whatever the point of sensitivity, mates should inform each other about their vulnerable spots, and then those should be "off limits" in an argument ("Please don't ever say that I don't care about my children"). To attack a mate at a sensitive point is like hitting below the belt; it is a deliberate effort to wound and hurt, rather than to improve the relationship. A mate has every right to cry "foul" when a vulnerability is struck.

Similarly, everyone has nonnegotiable limits, points of principle and realms of value which they will not surrender. The couple who cherish their relationship together will not violate those limits either by attacking them or by asking that they be given up. For example, I know a woman who loved her husband dearly and yet who discovered, after the birth of their first child, that the husband had exceedingly conservative and old-fashioned, stereotyped ideas about how children should be raised ("All boys should go out for football"; "It's sissy to be interested in music"). The woman was determined to let her children grow up, free of such stereotypes, and she therefore resisted every attempt by her husband to impose his preconceived notions on the children—that was the limit beyond which she would not negotiate. Fortunately her husband finally abandoned his attempts to invade her limits and adopted her point of view instead.

In marriages where the nonnegotiable limits of the couple are totally contradictory, it is practically impossible to achieve a compromise or a satisfactory accommodation. Very often such marriages split apart, if not actually physically then at least psychologically and spiritually, with both mates going their own separate ways. Beyond the achievement of open communication in marriage, there must be a reasonable correspondence between the couple's value structures. If basically they want different things, they will never achieve a close relationship, no matter how open and honest they may be with each other. Thus it is exceedingly important that each knows the values the other holds before they are wed.

The book of Ecclesiastes says that there is "a time to keep silence, and a time to speak; . . . a time for war, and a time for peace" (Eccl. 3:7–8). That certainly is true of family disagreements. There are times when it is appropriate to open an argument with a mate, and there are other times when it is absolutely disastrous. I sometimes wonder how many marriages are defeated by temporarily low blood-sugar levels! My husband and I have discovered that we should never make an important decision before breakfast, and we should never argue just before a meal: I never am fully awake before breakfast, and before meals, we both are tired and hungry and never very reasonable. The best time to argue or to discuss differences is when both are fully rested, wide awake, and feeling comfortably happy. Then it is amazing how rational and accommodating human beings can be.

In short, there is a discipline that must be imposed on conflict within a marriage if that conflict is to bear fruit and to contribute to the strengthening of the relationship. It is the couple who are totally committed to their relationship who are willing to impose such discipline on themselves. Wallace Denton has said, "For the most part, the way we handle anger is probably a learned behavior," [84] and the couple who value their relationship will learn to handle their anger in a fruitful fashion. They pick the right time to argue, they respect nonnegotiable limits and vulnerabilities, they argue only about what can be changed.

Further, they also know how to stick to the subject. The following argument really is going nowhere at all:

HE: You left the wheelbarrow out in the rain, and of course the wheel is rusted now. Why can't you *ever* learn to put things away when you're done with them?

SHE: Look who's talking! I pick up your dirty underwear and pajamas every morning of the week!

The wheelbarrow incident is generalized into a sweeping accusation. The wife is put on the defensive and launches her own counterattack, which has nothing to do with the original issue. There are at least two arguments involved here. Both could be dealt with rather simply and quickly, but only if each is discussed separately, and only if the mates are willing to accept responsibility. Suppose the conversation went like this:

HE: Honey, you left the wheelbarrow out in the rain last night.

SHE: Oh, no! I forgot all about it. I'm sorry. Did the wheel rust?

HE: Yeah.

SHE: Oh, gosh, is it ruined?

HE: No, I can clean off the rust and oil it up again, but I do wish you would remember to put things away after you're done with them.

SHE: I'm really sorry, honey. I will try to remember. I'm sorry I caused you the extra work.

HE: It's O.K., but do try to remember.

The incident with the wheelbarrow is closed (the underwear and pajamas belong in another discussion). The wife has acknowledged her responsibility, the husband has gained his end, there have been apology and forgiveness. Many arguments in marriage are as unimportant as this one and can easily be settled with responsibility and discipline on the part of both mates. Without those, such arguments over minor incidents can and often do balloon into serious altercations.

Included in a responsible and disciplined use of conflict is also the ability to listen carefully to the words of a mate and to be aware of the real issue. For example, many couples argue over money, but Wallace Denton has pointed out that conflicts over money can be an expression of many other deeper, unspoken issues.[85] A wife may complain that her husband does not give her enough money, when what she is really saying is that her husband does not care enough for her. Or a husband may complain that his wife has a separate bank account, when his real fear is that his wife does not think he is responsible. When couples fight, they need to make sure they are fighting over the actual issues involved. Only by listening to each other, by mutual questioning and leveling, can they get at those feelings which are really troubling them. Consider the following conversation:

HE: Don't tell me you're going to wear that dress to the party tonight!

SHE: What's the matter with this dress? You know I look good in it. You said so when I bought it.

HE: I didn't want to hurt your feelings, but frankly, you have lousy taste. Just look at those drapes you bought for the living room!

This fight is good for hours and a lot of tears, plus a rotten evening at the party. Suppose the husband did not attack his wife and his wife tried to get at the real issue involved:

HE: Is that the dress you're planning to wear to the party tonight?

SHE: I thought I might. Why? Don't you think I should?

HE: Well, this is a pretty important party at the boss's, honey, and I wonder if you shouldn't wear something more dressy.

or

I love you in that dress. It really makes you look sexy, but old Smitty is going to be there, and it bothers me when he starts eyeing you.

or

That dress is O.K., but I never liked it as well as your red one. That one really makes me feel proud of you.

The wife would have to change her dress, but she would have learned more about her husband, and a bitter argument would have been avoided by the lack of accusations and by getting at the real issues involved. In such simple fashion can a husband and wife learn the art of strengthening their relationship.

Third, the Christian couple who take as the pattern for their marriage God's relationships with his people know that finally the healing of every conflict is given with forgiveness.

Let us be as realistic as possible. Much argument in the home can be disciplined and responsible and lead to greater communication between mates, as I have tried to illustrate above. But there is also conflict within every marriage which is neither rational nor easily controlled. The angry outburst, the thoughtless and cutting remark, the seemingly unprovoked attack, the sharp retort—all issue forth from us at times, no matter how loving and intimate our marriage and regardless of how committed we are to it. Frail creatures of dust, we are all too subject to selfishness, to fatigue, to anxiety, to fear, to pride. These symptoms of our sinful nature break out in uncontrolled anger, disgust, and irritation. Indeed, the committed marriage is the one sphere within which we can unload our sinfulness safely, blowing off steam and releasing tensions. We can be what we are, sinful, selfish selves. Such is the truth in the popular motto from *Love Story*, "Love is never having to say you're sorry."

That is as far as the truth of that motto goes, however, because the ugly side of our natures awakens equally ugly sides in our mates. The angry outburst, the cutting remark, the attack or the retort, can call forth retaliating words from injured and dismayed partners. Words wound—even unintentionally—and once released, there is no way they can be recalled or wiped out. Like God's word, according to the prophet (Isa. 55:11), they do not return to us empty, but they unfortunately accomplish the purpose for which they were spoken, even when we wish they had not done so.

When our conflicts get out of control in our marriages, when we are fighting because we are sinful human beings, the only way the storm can be stilled is for one partner to break the cycle of mutual attack. If it is tit for tat, ugly word for ugly word, retaliation for hurt rendered, then there is no way the fight can be brought satisfactorily to an end. It will persist until all its damage is done, and it will affect the total climate of the marriage.

It is when such an ugly storm breaks out that forgiveness must be operative, the ability to accept a wound and to pardon and forget it, without seeking to retaliate for it or to store it up as a grudge. All marriage counselors are familiar with those persons who show up at their offices with long lists of stored-up grievances, sometimes even with dates and exact words committed to memory! Such offended souls may not have openly retaliated against their mates, but it is also certain that they have not forgiven them either. Unless real forgiveness is operative, the fight actually continues, if not in words then at least in feelings.

Forgiveness, in Christian marriage, is to be modeled after the forgiveness God offers us in Christ Jesus. Perhaps the clearest example we read of is Christ's forgiveness offered from the cross: "Father, forgive them; for they know not what they do" (Luke 23:34). Here forgiveness is offered despite the pain and suffering which have had to be borne. Forgiveness is honest acknowledgment that real wrong has been done. So too in the committed Christian marriage, there is clear-eyed recognition of sin—no phony or stoic telling oneself, "Well, it really didn't matter" or "No, I'm not really hurt" or "I probably had it coming." The Christian faith, amid all our rationalizations and self-justifications and side-steppings of responsibility for ourselves or others, realistically faces the fact that we do each other wrong. We need to realize that we wound each other terribly sometimes, by what we say or do. We violate the deepest feelings and trust of each other. We trample love into the ground, or, in the supreme violation, hang it on a cross. Forgiveness is the clear recognition that wrong has been done and therefore it must be dealt with in all its hideous reality.

Further, forgiveness as it is exercised by Christ is unconditional and uncalculating. Christ does not say, "I will die for you providing that you will reform and obey me," and he does not calculate what effect his forgiveness will have on us. He simply forgives and dies because of us and for us and on behalf of us, and thereby we know his love. So too with our mates: we are not to forgive

them only if they promise never to wrong us in the future
or only because we think it will restore peace. We are
simply to forgive, not to count their words or actions
against them in any sort of reckoning.

That means that forgiveness must always involve
forgetting. God tells us clearly in the words of the Old
Testament that he forgets our past sinful actions:

> I, I am He
> > who blots out your transgressions for my own sake,
> > and I will not remember your sins.
>
> > > > (Isa. 43:25.)

> I will forgive their iniquity, and I will remember their sin no
> more. (Jer. 31:34.)

In the New Testament, too, our past is forgotten by God.
Indeed, we are made new creatures in Christ. We are like
persons born again (cf. John 3:1–21). Our sin and errors
are wiped out. This is the meaning of II Cor. 5:17–19; let
us quote it again:

> If any one is in Christ, he is a new creation; *the old has passed
> away, behold, the new has come.* All this is from God, who
> through Christ reconciled us to himself and gave us the
> ministry of reconciliation; that is, God was in Christ reconcil-
> ing the world to himself, *not counting their trespasses against
> them,* and entrusting to us the message of reconciliation.
> (Italics added.)

Thus, forgiveness in marriage, if it is Christian forgiveness, is forgiveness which involves forgetting, which
cannot even remember the offenses a mate has committed, much less store them up and recount them later.

I know two women who consider themselves to be
loving wives. The first is elderly, but she still recounts
wrongs her husband did to her forty-five years ago. The
other, though young, can remember no specific grievance
against her husband if you ask her to name one. The
point is not that one husband has been more loving than

the other, but rather that one wife has forgiven and forgotten, while the other continues to remember. Forgiveness, according to the Biblical faith, means to blot past wrongs out of memory, because forgiveness is to be patterned after God's mercy, in which the past is fully forgotten and all things are made new.

Christian mates can exercise such forgiveness toward one another, because they know themselves constantly in need of it, and because they know they have time and again received such forgiveness when they did not deserve it. The love of Christ has flooded our hearts: that really is our motive-power for forgiveness. It does not come from ourselves and our own strength, but from his love poured out when he gave his life for us. He fills us with his spirit of forgiveness in order that we may forgive one another, and if we do not, we sin not only against one another but against his Holy Spirit (cf. Matt. 18:23–35). We are told to forgive one another seventy times seven (Matt. 18:21–22; cf. Luke 17:4), and if we do not, we do not and will not know the mercy of God toward us (cf. Matt. 6:12 and par.; 6:14–15; Mark 11:25–26). To refuse to forgive is to refuse to live in the power of the spirit of Christ, which is freely offered to us all.

Such forgiveness can break the cycle of mutual attack between mates in marriage. When one partner attacks, the other forgives and refuses to attack in turn. When an emotional wound is inflicted, no matter by what word or action, it is not returned in kind.

Such forgiveness can exercise a marvelous effect upon mates who are truly committed to strengthening their relationship. There are some "dirty and sick fighters" (Bach) of course, who will ignore its effects, who will continue in their raging monologues or accept love as their due, thinking that they are perfectly lovable no matter what they may do. But the Christian mates, who know themselves to be sinners in constant need of the forgiveness of Christ, will sooner or later recognize that they have wronged their marital partners by their angry words or faithless acts. Forgiveness and refusal to retaliate in the midst of an argument can bring a waiting calm, during which reason can return and the problem can be discussed. Sometimes a later phone call, after one partner has slammed angrily out of the house will be enough to say "I'm sorry" and to restore the peace of love. Sometimes a meek plea, "Can we be friends?" can take the place of words of reconciliation.

The point is that forgiveness brings with it repentance, if a couple are truly committed to their marriage. In the Christian faith it is not so much that we repent and are then forgiven, but that we are first forgiven and then repent, feeling truly sorry for our sins. The grace of love reforms us; the mercy of God renews our reason and wills, and because of God's love in Christ, we sincerely try to live a new and better life. So too is it in the marital relationship. When I am forgiven by my mate, I feel truly sorry for what I have done, and genuinely grateful that he nevertheless loves me and cares for me. Repentance and gratitude make me vow to try never to hurt him again. It is the forgiveness and grace which we know in love that make us say, "I'm sorry; I'll try not to do that again." Then the relationship is renewed and the trespass is forgotten. We have the chance to begin again in a deepened and more intimate relationship, which has been strengthened because it has conquered conflict by the power of forgiving love.

CHAPTER 11

Gifts of Extravagant Grace

Children, obey your parents in the Lord, for this is right. "Honor your father and mother" (this is the first commandment with a promise), "that it may be well with you and that you may live long on the earth." Fathers, do not provoke your children to anger, but bring them up in the discipline and instruction of the Lord.—Eph. 6:1–4

I sometimes think that children are the gift which is given out of the extravagance of God's grace. They are not absolutely necessary to a marital relationship. God fills our cup to the brim with his good gift of a mate for us, pouring out his love in his desire that we not be alone. Then, on top of that, he adds his marvelous gift of children. They become the overflow of his extravagance, the superabundance of blessing added to his original blessing (cf. Gen. 1:28), the final portion which makes our cup run over and magnifies our joy beyond all our original wishing. In Gen. 4:1, Eve sighs in contentment after the birth of Cain, "I have gotten a man with the help of the LORD." Many parents echo that certainty: children are a gift from God, out of the sheer extravagance of his love.

Such a view derives from faith in the life, death, and resurrection of Jesus Christ. In much of the Old Testament, children were by no means the extra measure added to marriage, but absolutely essential to it. The ancient Hebrew would go to extreme lengths to ensure that he had offspring (cf. Gen. 16:1 ff.; Deut. 25:5 ff.). Barrenness was understood as a result of God's curse (cf. Hos. 9:11–14), and the wife who could not bear children bore a special shame (cf. I Sam., ch. 1). The reasons are not hard to find. Israel had no doctrine of life after death until the second century B.C., and personal immortality was attainable only in the perpetuation of a man's name and personality in the person of his son. Further, God had promised that Israel would become a great nation (Gen. 12:2), and the multiplication of Israel's population was understood as a fulfillment of this divine promise and therefore a sign of divine favor. Because of the incarnation of Jesus Christ, however, the faithful—even when single or barren—may now be assured of eternal life. "Israel" has now become all those millions of every nation who confess their faith in the Son of God. Children now are not a necessity, either to a marriage or to the fulfillment of God's promise. But surely they are a marvelous superfluity!

That is a liberating word in our time, to know that children are not necessary to a marriage. Beyond the personal heartache of those who find they cannot have children, or the decisions of those who do not want them, our planet earth is becoming crowded with a surfeit of children. Our responsibility for subduing the earth and exercising dominion over it, given at the time of creation (Gen. 1:28), now has to be held in careful balance with our ability to "be fruitful and multiply." The problem is not only that we will run out of food, but also literally out of space, and we recoil in horror before the problems of shelter, pollution, and disease that a dense and impoverished population can—and now is—introducing into the world. Theologian Roger Shinn pointed out before a Senate hearing some years ago that unless we take responsibility for limiting world population, it will automatically limit itself through war and famine and disease. Surely responsible birth control presents the more merciful means of limitation. So to hear that we need not have children is a liberating word. More and more couples are exercising that freedom by limiting their offspring to one or two, or by adopting someone else's children.

Nevertheless, children are a marvelous superfluity, the frosting on our cake of matrimonial bliss! Just think of the gifts they come trailing after them: the ability to transcend our own finitude—to see the world through their eyes and so to enlarge it and our learning; to relive in some measure our own past as children and to participate in the future through them; above all, to watch and guide and have a hand in the development of the miracle which is the human personality, from the moment of conception to the time of maturity. I would not trade anything in the world for the opportunity of knowing our son and daughter. Sometimes I wonder if those women who are crying so loudly for "abortion on demand" really understand the magnitude of the deprivation they are inflicting, not only on the human race as a whole but also on themselves. Some abortion is no doubt necessary and merciful, but much of it among middle-class Americans is being perpetrated only for convenience's sake.

Heaven knows it is never wholly convenient to have children! From the moment of their conception, until the day we die, they change our lives drastically. Let no young couple cherish the fantasy that children will not alter their lives and marriages and take up huge amounts of their time, their concern, and their money! Those young ones are carried home from the hospital, looking so small and feeble, whimpering and totally helpless, and lacking in all power. God gives us children as the overflow of his grace, and then works through them in power to make us persons we never dreamed we would become.

Think of the things God teaches us through the channels of our children! The first lesson is one in humility, proper to the dependent creatures that we are. A childless couple may delude themselves into thinking they are mature and self-controlled, but we parents soon discover in relation to our children that we are far from any such perfection. We become angry at that tiny helpless infant lying in his crib because he is "perverse" enough to sleep all day and cry all night. We lose complete patience with our elementary-schoolers because they seem to have nothing better to do than to bicker with one another. We experience agonies of frustration over our inability to teach our adolescents to listen. We find ourselves powerless to steer our young married offspring away from wrong decisions. Somehow in relations with our children, we parents are brought face to face with our own terrible limitations—our inability always to love, to keep our tempers, to understand, to enter into another's viewpoint, to convince and guide by reason. We are brought quite existentially to confrontation with sinful depths in ourselves that we never knew existed. For a Christian, that can be a very helpful experience, a signpost on the way to healing and personal wholeness.

In relation to our children, we parents also become vividly aware of the limits of our wisdom. There are so many situations in child-rearing which do not present us with a clear-cut choice between good and bad alternatives. Should we force Suzy to take piano lessons? Should Johnny be allowed certain friends? Should Bill go to private school or remain at home in a poorer one? Has Tom made the wisest vocational choice? Should Sally marry now? Have we guided properly, instilled the right values, prepared adequately for the future? The fact is that we parents are never completely sure if we have or not. We become quite conscious that we are not all-wise and that in many situations we do not know the one right thing to do. It is a valuable lesson for us human beings to learn, who are so ready to make ourselves gods and to chart our own destiny (cf. Gen., chs. 3; 11). We think sometimes we can run our own lives. Our children can teach us that, after all, we do need a Master, a love and wisdom beyond our own limited capacities.

Beyond humbling us, however, the experience of parenthood can greatly increase our self-respect and our knowledge of our own capacity for good and self-sacrifice. To use Roger Mehl's phrase, parenthood brings with it "manifold servitudes." When our children are little, there are a thousand and one tasks that must be performed in service to them—not only the routines of infancy, of bathing and feeding and changing diapers. In a way, these are the simplest jobs. Later on come the tasks of bandaging knees, picking up toys, blowing runny noses, answering questions, mediating disputes, entertaining, helping, educating, guiding. Our serenity and routine are interrupted, our daily plans punctured by our children. Once we have offspring, our life is never quite all our own again.

The amazing thing, however, is that we parents grow with our servitude, and we find ourselves capable of doing things we never knew we could do. We find we have amazing stores of patience and understanding when our love for our children prompts us to minister to their trouble or hurt. We find we *can* go sleepless when a child is sick, we *can* love someone who is acting in a completely unlovable manner, we *can* give up possessions or plans for the sake of our children's welfare. Our children call forth from us an astounding store of competence, maturity, and goodness. Our love for them enables us to become persons we never could have become had we not been required to serve their needs and rights. Surely God works through his gift of children to make us the persons he intends!

Of course there is nothing in parenthood that forces us to accept the humility, the knowledge of ourselves, and the maturity that God can give us through our children, just as there is nothing in the gospel that ever coerces us into accepting new life. We all know people who reject God's gifts through children. Some of them remain completely selfish all their lives, and for that reason decide not to have children at all—a rationale totally different from legitimate concern for the problems of overpopulation. Consider the following argument by a woman reporter, printed some years ago in *The Saturday Evening Post*:

> . . . [My husband and I] enjoy our life and the things we do singly and together. We appreciate the time and freedom to pursue potential talents. . . . We treasure the freedom to pick up and disappear for a weekend or a month or even a year, to sleep odd hours, to breakfast at three A.M. or three P.M., to hang out the DO NOT DISTURB sign, to slam a door and be alone, or alone together . . . to tease and love anywhere, any hour, anytime we please without a nagging guilt that a child is being neglected. We take so small a privilege as privacy for granted; yet, to our friends with children, privacy is a luxury for which they envy us. . . .
>
> I see so many of our friends, some of them with children they hadn't necessarily planned on—bitter, frustrated, vacillating between devotion and despair, screaming at their youngsters, tearing into each other. The child is there. Never for a moment would they wish it away, but they seem to be fighting a furious battle as they watch themselves becoming people they never meant to be. . . .
>
> The more we watch our contemporaries trying to cope with child-rearing, the more we see them bowing to its conflicting demands and surrendering their individualities and dreams, the stronger our decision to remain childless becomes.[86]

When we read such a statement, we can only reply, "Well, thank God, so be it." Such an attitude should surely disqualify those who hold it from entering the ranks of parenthood. This is not to say that we who are parents never feel the harassment and frustration pictured above. But perhaps the basic lesson our children teach us—indeed, sometimes force upon us—is that love consists in the willingness to take the time and trouble to be concerned about someone besides ourselves. In Jesus Christ, we see one who was willing to be completely troubled for our sakes, and our children teach us willingly to shoulder that burden of troubled love. It is a wonderful gift, because no one enslaves us quite as much as we do ourselves. In our love and concern for our children we are mercifully given one of God's ways for loosing those slavish bonds.

Some parents resent the sacrifice and price that their children cost them. These are the parents who demand that their children "repay" them: the aged mother who thinks her grown children never pay enough attention to her, the father who feels his son has ungratefully turned away from his ideals and standards: "I work hard to build up this business, and then he doesn't have one bit of interest in it!" So runs the complaint of the parent who wants to be repaid. But love is never repaid; it is only loved in return.

In similar fashion, there will always be those parents who refuse to learn humility, who will always maintain their own rightness in relation to their children. Some of them in fact will demand that theirs is "the way, and the truth, and the life" which their children must follow. They will either smother their child into submission to them or reject him or her for refusing to knuckle under to their will. We know these souls too. They are the fathers who require their sons to attend their alma maters, the mothers who reject the boy who is "not good enough" for their daughter, the parents who mete out unjust punishment because their wills have been contradicted. Such parents have made themselves gods over their children, with no knowledge of their own limitations and shortcomings. They are illustrations of the fact that parenthood without God can become a demonic substitute for divinity.

It takes a lot of faith to be a parent. Not surprisingly, that has always been so. Sometimes we meet couples who are unwilling to have children, because the world now is too chaotic or its future too uncertain. But some of the early church fathers advanced similar arguments: they thought the world was soon going to be destroyed.[87] Perhaps bringing children into the world then, as into the chaos of our present disorder, seemed an exercise in foolhardy optimism. But the basic fact for the Christian is that the future of the world is not at all uncertain. It lies in God's hands and moves toward his goal, as it always has, and the parents who rest their trust in that fact can raise their offspring in certain joy.

> God is our refuge and strength,
>   a very present help in trouble.
> Therefore we will not fear though the earth
>   should change,
>   though the mountains shake in the heart
>   of the sea.
>
> (Ps. 46:1-2.)

Thus could the psalmist sing, as the void of chaos threatened his world too. And thus we Christian parents still can sing in this atomic age:

> Lift up your eyes to the heavens,
>   and look at the earth beneath;
> for the heavens will vanish like smoke,
>   the earth will wear out like a garment,
>   and they who dwell in it will die like
>   gnats;

but my salvation will be for ever,
and my deliverance will never be ended.
(Isa. 51:6.)

It is that "but" at the end of the verse that makes all the difference. God rules, abides, and delivers, though we blow this world off its axis. That has always been the only hope that humankind ever had. It is still the hope that makes fearless parenthood possible in an age such as ours.

Some sincere Christians refuse to have children because they feel inadequate. "We don't think we are good enough to be parents," goes the reasoning. "We would be sure to make too many mistakes and ruin our child for life." Part of this attitude has been fostered by a misunderstanding of the findings of modern psychology. Some parents anxiously think that if they mishandle junior's thumb-sucking problem, they have marked him indelibly. They take upon themselves the *total* responsibility for how their child turns out, believing that the development of his character and his ultimate success or failure are the results only of what they do. They forget completely that their child is influenced by a thousand seen and unseen forces in the community, and they therefore suffer under a staggering load of anxiety and sometimes eventual guilt.

There is no doubt that we do partially influence our children, and unfortunately, we do instill in them our own imperfect ways. When it comes right down to it, none of us is "good enough" to be a parent. By the most subtle methods, by everything we do, our imperfect personalities shape and mold to some extent the personalities of our offspring. We pass on to them our fears, our prejudices, our hatreds. Our anxieties and stresses sometimes even show up in their physical health, and Johnny has asthma or Mary stutters because of what we are.

We want so much to love our children perfectly. We do not want to become angry with them and to yell at them

for some misdoing. We do not want to become impatient
with their failure to understand. We do not want to
punish them unjustly simply to relieve our own feelings.
But we do these things. What we manifest toward our
offspring is not perfect love but our own sinful humanity.
We feel guilty and troubled by these failures to show love
to the very persons whom we feel we love from the
depths of our beings. No, none of us is "good enough" to
be a parent; "none is righteous, no, not one" (Rom. 3:10).

Nevertheless, God turns over to us the power to
propagate and to have children, the power to share in his
creative act. Just as the sinful, weak, inadequate nation
of Israel was chosen to be the instrument of God's
revelation in the world, so we sinful, weak, inadequate
persons are chosen to be parents and God's shepherds of
the young. As God puts this fearful responsibility into
our hands, at the same time he encompasses us about
once more with a marvelous mercy. He works in the lives
of our children. Beyond our fumbling and bumbling,
beyond our misdirection and sinful guidance, God shapes
and molds our children's lives and uses them to his good
purpose. We may not be adequate to bring up our
children, but God always is, and he never deserts them or
forgets about them or leaves them out of his sight.
Trusting that guidance, believing that God will use even
our mistakes with our children, we parents have the
courage to continue in our stewardship.

Even more, we parents can raise our children free from
anxiety and guilt, because we know that in Jesus Christ
we are forgiven our blind errors and sinful wrong.
Indeed, it is precisely through the instrument of our
children that God often extends to us his forgiveness.
Every parent has had the experience of unjustly pun-
ishing a child: we become tired and crotchety and whack
a child on the behind, not so much because the child has
been bad, but mostly to relieve our own feelings. What

happens? Two minutes later, our child is hugging us and kissing us and saying, "I love you, Mommy," and in that instant we know we have been forgiven for our sinful past. The wrong we have done has not been held against us. It has been forgotten in love. We have the possibility of starting over, of making a new beginning. Through our children themselves, we are offered the healing of forgiveness. All things are made new in such forgiveness and that makes parenting possible.

In the task of educating and disciplining our children, then, perhaps one of the most important things we can do is to learn how to admit to our children that we have been in error. There are some parents who can never bring themselves to say "I was wrong" or "I am sorry" to their child. They think this somehow shows a weakness on their part, and they never want to admit to their child that they can make a mistake. But children must learn that parents too can err, for this teaches them three valuable lessons.

In the first place, a parent's confession of error teaches a child that no one is sinless. In the eyes of our little children, we *are* akin to gods—all-powerful, all-knowing, all-wise, and good. As our children grow, however, they must learn that we are not gods and that we too are dependent on our heavenly Father. By the confession of our wrong, our children learn that no one is good except God. Thereby they come to understand themselves and their world in a realistic fashion.

Second, if we are able to apologize to our children, they begin to learn that forgiveness forms the fabric which holds people together. They see that an error or a transgression is not the end of a relationship and that it can be overcome and made void by forgiveness and reconciliation. They begin to understand the basis of Christian marriage and community, and they are prepared, by human example, for their relationship with God.

Third, by asking pardon from our children we strengthen their sense of right and wrong. Children know ' very well when they have suffered an injustice. They can spot an unfairness or an abuse in the family often before we parents become aware of anything we have done amiss. If we do not confess that we have been unfair or that we have committed some error, our children begin to doubt their own moral judgments. They become confused about just what is right and wrong. Finally they begin to rationalize their own behavior as they have seen their parents do. If we parents break the family moral code, we have to admit it, or after a while that code will become meaningless for our children.

None of the foregoing should be misunderstood, however. The willingness to acknowledge our sins and to learn from our children should not be distorted into a refusal to exercise authority over them in their training and discipline. There is something perversely misguided about those families run strictly as a "democracy," with the children possessing an equal vote in decision-making with the parents. Children should not be expected to possess wisdom and maturity equal to that of their parents. To refuse to guide and discipline them is not only to lay burdens upon them which they really cannot bear, but it is also sinfully to refuse to accept our God-given responsibilities as parents.

Some parents, misguided by popularized psychology, are terribly afraid that if they say "No" to a child, they will injure his or her personality. Or they are afraid that if they hinder him or her, the child will become frustrated. Or they fear that to exercise parental authority will lead the child not to like them.

Psychiatrist Joseph Noshpitz has pointed out that there are numerous reasons why parents avoid disciplining their children.[88] Some cannot say "No" to a child because they cannot say "No" to themselves. A few actually think their child's aberrant behavior is "cute" or makes their child "interesting" or "outstanding." Others become totally passive toward their child because they want to have "peace at any price": when father gets home from the office, he wants to relax with his newspaper; he does not want to be disturbed and have to bother with behavior problems. Actually it is the undisciplined child who will never give the parent any peace. As Prov. 29:17 puts it, "Discipline your son, and he will give you rest; he will give delight to your heart" (cf. Prov. 29:15). Parents who postpone discipline simply guarantee trouble for themselves in the future. As Noshpitz has pointed out:

> A home that has no taboos, that makes no demands, that requires no politeness or conformity, that sets no firm rules and limits, is a home that the city sanitary inspector ought to serve a ticket to. It's an unhealthy place, a breeding ground for trouble. And trouble there will be. A child's character needs adequate structure, and to begin with, these controls must come from without. Only when the external controls have been adequate can the child take them into himself, make them part of himself, and thus have the necessary internal structure to allow growth to proceed fully and well.[89]

If we love our children, if we truly want them to live full and abundant lives, if we deeply wish them to become all that God created them to become, then we will continually train and discipline them. It is significant that the Biblical writers have very little to say about children, but what they do say largely involves these two basic needs of every child—the need to be loved in a home and the need to be trained.

Some of the classic pictures of parental love are found in the Old Testament. Despite the fact that Hebrew culture was totally different from ours, those pictures evoke emotions with which every parent can identify. What father cannot sympathize with the weeping David, who has just heard that his son Absalom has been killed, and who, stunned and grieving, gropes his way toward a private place where he can mourn unashamedly: "O my son Absalom, my son, my son Absalom! Would I had died instead of you, O Absalom, my son, my son!" (II Sam. 18:33)? Or what mother, whose children have somehow slipped away from her, does not know Rachel's sorrow?

> A voice is heard in Ramah,
>   lamentation and bitter weeping.
> Rachel is weeping for her children;
>   she refuses to be comforted for her children,
>   because they are not.
>
>   (Jer. 31:15.)

As parents, we all know what Abraham must have felt on that long walk to the land of Moriah to sacrifice Isaac, "your son, your only son, whom you love" (Gen. 22:1–19). The writer tells us twice for emphasis that "they went both of them together" (Gen. 22:6, 8); they walk in silence except for those gentle words, "My father!" and "Here am I, my son" (Gen. 22:7). Fathers and sons, mothers and children—those words speak deep emotions in the Bible, so deep that God himself is known as "Father" and the illustration of his love for us can be put in the form of a story about a wandering son and a waiting father (Luke 15:11–32), or in the form of sayings about a mother:

> Can a woman forget her sucking child,
>   that she should have no compassion
>   on the son of her womb?
> Even these may forget,
>   yet I will not forget you.
>
>   (Isa. 49:15.)

> As one whom his mother comforts,
>   so I will comfort you;
>   you shall be comforted in Jerusalem.
>   (Isa. 66:13.)

Or finally this:

> If you then, who are evil, know how to give good gifts to your children, how much more will your Father who is in heaven give good things to those who ask him! (Matt. 7:11 and par.)

Both Old Testament and New know the love we parents have for our children, and use that love to give us a sense of God's love for us.

In the Biblical perspective, true parental love, however, always includes within its definition, our willingness to train and discipline our children. Proverbs' stern admonitions are now out of date in their methods of discipline (Prov. 22:15; 23:13)—from them came the old saying, "Spare the rod and spoil the child." But it is significant that we altered that saying somewhere along the line. What Prov. 13:24 really says is, "He who spares the rod *hates* his son, but he who loves him is diligent to discipline him." Discipline is an integral part of love, and it is this emphasis in the saying which remains of permanent validity.

The Biblical faith presents a profound understanding of what child discipline is. It can perhaps best be summed up in the words of Eph. 6:4: "Fathers, do not provoke your children to anger, but bring them up in the discipline and instruction of the Lord." There are a training and a teaching which come from God, and throughout the Bible, these are to be passed on to our children.

> My son, do not despise the LORD's discipline
>   or be weary of his reproof,
> for the LORD reproves him whom he loves,
>   as a father the son in whom he delights.
> (Prov. 3:11–12.)

Deuteronomy emphasizes over and over again that we are to teach our children what God has done and said (Deut. 4:9–10; 6:7, 20 ff.; 11:18–19; 31:12–13), and Proverbs urges that such training start at an early age (Prov. 19:18), because it is decisive (Prov. 22:6).

What is this "discipline and instruction of the Lord," which both Testaments are so concerned about? It is not synonymous with punishment. Rather, it could perhaps best be characterized by the word "responsibility"; for example, in Deut. 8:5, God's discipline of Israel in the desert is a test of their responsibility to him. To bring up our children "in the nurture and admonition of the Lord," to use the old phraseology, is to teach them that they are responsible to God, not only in the religious sphere, but in every area of their lives. There was no separation between secular and sacred in Biblical thought. Religious education was education for life, and the basic content of that education is to train our children to know and practice their accountability to their Creator.

As Karl Menninger has so cogently pointed out in his book *Whatever Became of Sin?*,[90] a lack of a sense of responsibility is probably the greatest weakness of our society today. No one will accept responsibility anymore for any of society's evils—for crime, for pollution, for waste, for poverty, for ignorance, for violence, for oppression. It is always someone else who has perpetrated these evils, not we. "They" are responsible, and "they" should do something about it. We have even lost the vocabulary of responsibility. We no longer talk of "sin," but of "crime" or of "mental illness" or of "symptoms" of sickness, and those are controlled, not by taking responsibility, but by enlarging the police force and adding to the staff of mental institutions and hospitals. As individuals, we do not say we have sinned; we say we have "goofed," and so we excuse ourselves lightly. "Sorry about that" is the closest we come to accepting responsibility for our actions. Otherwise we blame what we do on the way we were raised, or on the nature of society, or on some psychological hang-up we have, which makes us act as we do. We thereby lose the basic nature of our humanity.

It is characteristic of human beings in the Biblical faith that they are accountable to God. In that profound picture in Gen., ch. 3, first Adam and then Eve try to "pass the buck": "The woman whom thou gavest to be with me, she gave me fruit of the tree, and I ate" (Gen.

3:12); "The serpent beguiled me, and I ate" (Gen. 3:13); "Lord, it's not our fault," is what the primal couple are saying. But God does not accept our excuses or our attempts to escape responsibility. "What is this that you have done?" is always his question to us (Gen. 3:13). When Cain, in the following story of Gen., ch. 4, disavows all responsibility for his brother (Gen. 4:9), God again asks that uncomfortable question, "What have you done?" (Gen. 4:10). The nature of the human personality is that we must answer to our Creator, and when we try to escape that answerability, we become something less than human.

So it is that in the discipline and training of our children, we are called upon to teach them that they are responsible, not only to themselves, their families, and their society, but above all to God. When my three brothers and I were growing up, our mother had two Bible verses which she kept always before us. One was from Proverbs: "In all thy ways acknowledge him, and he shall direct thy paths" (Prov. 3:6, KJV), a saying that has proved repeatedly true through the years. The other was a saying of our Lord: "Every one to whom much is given, of him will much be required" (Luke 12:48). We were, Mother said, given many talents, opportunities, abilities, and goods, but precisely because we had been given these things by our Creator, he held us responsible for using them wisely and fully. A talent for music could not be wasted; it had to be put to practice daily. An ability to learn in school had to be matched by devotion to homework. A comfortable living standard brought its requirement of sharing with others. Nothing we had was of our doing or making; it was a gift of a loving Creator, and thus bore with it a responsibility to use it wisely and well. So we always stood under the "discipline and instruction" of the Lord.

Mother also opened our minds to what the will of God

was by reading to us from the Scriptures. Deuteronomy repeatedly emphasizes this teaching function of parents, and fathers should note that many of the Biblical admonitions concerning the education of children are specifically directed to males. In this age of commuter trains and jets, many fathers have abandoned their role as a teacher of their children, leaving it up to the mother, or sometimes to the child himself. In his book, *Christians in Families*,[91] Roy Fairchild asks what would happen if a man from Mars came to our door and told one of our children, "Take me to your leader." To whom would the child turn? To the father? To the mother? Or would he say he was his own leader? The questions are pointedly relevant to our family situations, and perhaps every parent, especially every father, needs to ask them of himself.

The corollary of this Biblical emphasis on our God-given responsibility for the education of our children is an equal emphasis on the necessity for children to obey.

> Hear, my son, your father's instruction,
>   and reject not your mother's teaching;
> for they are a fair garland for your head,
>   and pendants for your neck.
>   (Prov. 1:8–9; cf. 6:20; 10:1.)

In Col. 3:20 the writer urges, "Children, obey your parents in everything, for this pleases the Lord," and in Eph. 6:1: "Children, obey your parents in the Lord, for this is right." Significantly, Eph. 6:4 adds, "Fathers, do not provoke your children to anger . . . ," an admonition quite similar to Col. 3:21: "Fathers, do not provoke your children, lest they become discouraged." There is recognition in the New Testament that parents must deserve respect, that the actions and attitudes of parents toward their children must inspire obedience.

Nevertheless it is clear that one of the lessons which children must be taught is respect and honor for parents, yet finally it is only the parents themselves who can teach that lesson. There is something drastically wrong in a home when the authority and honor of parents are not acknowledged. The eight-year-old who sasses his elders, the adolescent who is allowed always to contradict his father, the preschooler who gets away without punishment when he repeatedly hits or sticks out his tongue at his mother are known to us all. They represent that widespread breed which has been taught nothing of the Bible's honor for parents (Ex. 20:12; Deut. 5:16). "I remember still," writes Phyllis McGinley, "the patient, the wistful voice of a woman sitting next to me in the park not so long ago. 'Mother wishes you wouldn't,' she was repeating monotonously to her frail four-year-old. 'Mother doesn't like to be hit in the head with a dump truck.' " [92] The prophets would maintain that such a scene is a symptom of chaos in society.

When Ezekiel wishes to portray the sickness of Israelite society, he points to the fact that "father and mother are treated with contempt in you" (Ezek. 22:7), and Isaiah writes of the collapse of Israel's life this way:

> I will make boys their princes,
>   and babes shall rule over them.
> And the people will oppress one another,
>   every man his fellow
>   and every man his neighbor;
> the youth will be insolent to the elder,
>   and the base fellow to the honorable.
> (Isa. 3:4–5.)

Children must be educated to enter cooperatively and willingly into a family community which took shape before they appeared. This is one of the reasons why it is important for a husband and wife to have some years alone together before the birth of their first child. They must first establish that community of the home into which the child is then trained to take a place. Once having done this, the foundation is laid for the child to accept himself or herself and subsequently to find his or her role in the larger community of society. As a friend once humorously remarked: "Our children are born savages. Our job is to civilize them."

Unfortunately, many homes are centered completely around the child's needs and wants. Instead of educating a child to share, to work cooperatively, to have respect for the needs and wants of others, too often out of our superabundance, we provide everything he or she desires. If there is a conflict over which television program to watch, we buy the child a television set. If an adolescent is monopolizing the phone, we provide another phone. As a result, the child never learns to consider the other person. Such a child is what the psychologists call "overgratified." Later when the child matures and ventures forth in the world and seeks a marriage partner, such a person invariably looks for the mate who will gratify every wish, as the parents have done. As Dr. Noshpitz remarks, "What marital problems *that* can make for later on!" [93] Training, discipline, responsibility, education into a family group—these are absolutely essential if our children are to be raised "in the discipline and instruction of the Lord."

Just as children need some limits structured into their conduct, so too parents need some limits on their exercise of authority. These finally come from the convictions of faith. Our children do not belong to us. They belong to God. And when we realize that, we know we cannot impose our will or our society's will completely on our children. For example, we cannot ask that our child enter only one particular profession, or we cannot insist that he or she share our society's standards of "success." We cannot even demand that a child be completely "normal," when that normality is defined as nothing more than conformity to the current mores. Our child, after all, may reject society's standards and our ways as inadequate.

The career of every prophet in the Bible embodies such rejection of the *status quo*. Insofar as a person acts responsibly toward God and fellow human beings, he or she must be given the freedom to engage in such rejection. Both we and our society are imperfect and sinful in God's eyes, and whenever we believe that and act upon it, we leave room for the freedom of nonconformity. Faith refuses to absolutize the present, and it recognizes that the conduct to which our children are prepared and called by God may be new departures from old and accepted ways. The parent who believes in God must be the flexible parent, who is willing to let God do a "new thing" through his or her children's lives.

In the same manner, if we believe we do not possess our children, we then have the willingness to let them go, to give them freedom from us, once we have trained and educated them to the limits of our ability. There is an old saying that "mother love is wonderful," but as Clark Ellzey has pointed out, that is not necessarily true: "Some mother love can be the most frightening thing in the life of a child." [94] It may smother a child and refuse to let him grow into an independent person. Or it may manipulate a child, to relieve its own feelings of pride or power or frustration. While they are little, our children are completely dependent on our love and approval for their sense of security and self-worth, and some parents begin to manipulate their children, by giving or withholding love. By doing such a thing, we turn ourselves into false gods for our children and deny that it is the Lord's purpose and not ours to which they are ultimately responsible.

Since the death of my own mother, I think perhaps one of my greatest impoverishments is that of no longer having her prayers on my behalf. We children never asked Mother if she prayed for us, but we all knew she did—day in, day out, through the years. We also knew that those prayers had guided us in paths we otherwise might not have taken, delivered us from temptation to which we otherwise might have fallen victim, infused our lives with a grace that we otherwise might never have known. Mother realized fully that we were not really her children or Dad's, but God's alone. Daily she lifted us up before our Father in her prayers and asked his guidance and protection of us.

I cannot help thinking that perhaps finally that is what parenting is all about: to receive our beloved children as the gift of God's extravagant grace, to bring them up in his discipline and instruction, asking constantly his working and guidance beyond our own limited wisdom and understanding, and then to rest content, knowing that our children's lives are "hid with Christ in God" (Col. 3:3). He will bring them to their good end, in the fulfillment of his loving purpose.

Notes

1. Such is the meaning of the Hebrew text.
2. *Ibid.*
3. Shana Alexander, quoting an interview with Liv Ullmann, about her role as Nora in Henrik Ibsen's *A Doll's House,* in a column entitled "Beyond the Doll's House," *Newsweek,* Feb. 17, 1975, p. 100.
4. The celibacy of priests and nuns in the Roman Catholic Church has, for centuries, born powerful witness to man's final responsibility to God rather than to the world, and from a practical standpoint has provided the Roman Church with great flexibility in the support and placement of its leaders. Unfortunately, however, influenced by early Patristic emphases on the evil nature of the body, the Roman Church has maintained that the celibate life is more perfect and pleasing to God than is the life of the married person. Such a view cannot be supported from the Scriptures and is now being widely challenged by clergy and laity within the Roman Catholic Church itself. How the Holy See will ultimately respond to such challenge under the reign of the next pope remains to be seen.

The following is a good summary of the Roman Catholic views regarding celibacy:

"Virginity or celibacy is more excellent than marriage. This is a dogma of faith.

"The reasons for which it is embraced are to think of the Lord, to be more entirely devoted to His service or to the good of our neighbor, to realize more numerous advantages for advancement in the spiritual life. The underlying motive for all this is a preference of love. For it is out of love for Christ that one undertakes this way of life.

"Perfect chastity effects a spiritual marriage between the soul and Christ.

"Perfect chastity deserves the name of the angelic virtue since it is an eschatological state or way of life anticipating here on earth the life that all of us will be obliged (and privileged) to live in eternity. Thus those who have vowed their chastity to God are signs or images (especially in the case of women) of the perfect integrity of the union between Christ and the Church.

"While the state of perfect chastity is not a sacrament and does not confer grace *ex opere operato*, still it does afford those who embrace it something spiritual which far exceeds the mutual helps which married persons confer upon each other. The personality of those who take this way of life upon themselves does not suffer harm; rather it gains immensely. For God shares with these persons His own divine life in a more abundant manner.

"The fruits of virginity and celibacy are many, especially with regard to the sanctification of souls. Thus, far from abdicating fatherhood or motherhood, those who embrace this way of life increase it immensely, since they beget not for an earthly and transitory life but for the heavenly and eternal one. A deeper faith and holiness and the wonderful example which they afford to the whole Church are likewise to be enumerated among the fruits arising from this practice.

"Priests are to encourage vocations to these walks of life, and parents are also to willingly offer to the service of God those of their sons and daughters who feel called to it. They are not to interfere with a vocation in any way but consider it a great honor to see their son elevated to the priesthood or their daughter consecrate her life to God.

"Although marriage is inferior to dedicated chastity, we are not to conclude that marriage is an evil. Nor is virginity or chastity necessary for Christian perfection. Holiness of life can be attained even without chastity that is consecrated to God. Marriage, therefore, is a good, but a lesser good than the life of chastity consecrated to God.

"Virginity is something that is not of precept but rather of counsel. Hence it demands free choice and supernatural help and assistance from God." (Charles A. Schleck, C.S.C., *The Sacrament of Matrimony*, pp. 265–266; The Bruce Publishing Company, 1964.)

5. As stated in a lecture by Dr. Edmund Schlink, Heidelberg University, Germany, 1952.

6. Cf. Paul's defense of his actions over against the criticisms of the Corinthians (I Cor. 4:3–5).

7. Carl R. Rogers, in *Becoming Partners: Marriage and Its Alternatives* (Dell Publishing Co., Inc., 1972), gives a good selection.

8. Paul recognizes the power of sexual drives (I Cor. 7:8–9), and yet marriage based on lust is specifically forbidden in I Thess. 4:3–8.

9. The official Roman Catholic view of marriage still holds that procreation and education of the children form the primary purposes of marriage. Pius XII stated this view in an address to the Italian Catholic Union of Midwives on October 29, 1951: "The truth is that marriage, as a natural institution, by virtue of the will of the Creator has not as a primary and intimate end the personal perfecting of the couples, but the procreation and education of new life. . . . Does this mean that we deny or diminish what there is of good and right in the personal values arising from marriage and its carrying out? Certainly not. . . . But it must not be divorced from the primary function of marriage which is service for new life. Not only the common work of external life but also intellectual and spiritual endowment, even the depths of spirituality in conjugal love as such, have been put by the will of nature and the Creator at the service of our descendants." (As quoted by Schleck, *op. cit.*, p. 31.)

10. As stated in a discussion by David and Vera Mace, at Union Theological Seminary in Virginia, February 4, 1975. Also see their book, *We Can Have Better Marriages If We Really Want Them* (Abingdon Press, 1974).

11. Cf. the case of Gail and Dick, reported in Rogers, *Becoming Partners,* especially pp. 36–39.

12. *Richmond Times-Dispatch,* March 6, 1975, p. D-12.

13. As quoted in the Lancaster, Pa. *Intelligencer-Journal,* Dec. 27, 1961, p. 6. This quote is still very typical of the American business scene.

14. Rogers, *Becoming Partners,* p. 200.

15. *The Book of Common Prayer,* 1944.

16. See, for example, many of the case studies in Rogers, *Becoming Partners.*

17. *Ibid.,* pp. 142–143.

18. *Ibid.,* p. 158.

19. David and Vera Mace, *op. cit.,* p. 25.

20. *Ibid.,* p. 107.

21. *Newsweek,* March 23, 1970, p. 74.

22. Roxanne Dunbar, in Mary Lou Thompson (ed.), *Voices of the New Feminism* (Beacon Press, Inc., 1970), p. 46.

23. *Newsweek,* March 23, 1970, p. 73.

24. *Ibid.*

25. Betty Friedan, in Thompson (ed.), *op. cit.,* p. 32.

26. *Ibid.,* p. 38.

27. *New York Times* News Service, Oct. 3, 1974.

28. Erwin D. Canham, *National Manpower Council* (Columbia University Press, 1958), pp. 13–14.

29. Sylvia Porter. Field Enterprises, Inc., Feb. 21, 1975.

30. *Newsweek,* March 23, 1970, p. 75.

31. Cynthia Wedel, *Employed Women and the Church* (National Council of the Churches of Christ in the U.S.A., 1959).

32. Sylvia Porter. Field Enterprises, Inc.

33. Thompson (ed.), *op. cit.,* p. 107.

34. Nancy Seifer. Anderson-Moberg Syndicates, Inc., Jan. 26, 1975.

35. Joseph Noshpitz, "Why Discipline Is So Vital in Helping Children to Grow," *The National Observer,* May 16, 1966, p. 22.

36. Friedan, in Thompson (ed.), *op. cit.,* pp. 34–35.

37. Elizabeth Duncan Koontz, in *ibid.,* pp. 85–86.

38. Alice S. Rossi, in *ibid.,* p. 70.

39. *Newsweek,* March 23, 1970, p. 75.

40. As reported in a column by Henry J. Taylor, *Richmond Times-Dispatch,* May 14, 1975, p. A-14.

41. Sara Martin Wolfe, "Letters to the Editor," *The National Observer,* April 12, 1965. This letter is still very typical of the attitude of many persons.

42. Mary Daly, *Beyond God the Father: Toward a Philosophy of Women's Liberation* (Beacon Press, Inc., 1973).

43. Mary Daly, *The Church and the Second Sex* (Harper & Row, Publishers, Inc., 2d ed., 1975).

44. *Ibid.,* p. 17.

45. Susan Ross Clewell, Anita Herrick, Susan Halverstadt, Susan Vogel, Susan Thornton, "Women Theologizing: Naming and Claiming Our Style," *Theological Education,* Winter 1975, p. 81.

46. *Ibid.,* p. 79.

47. Technically, we are created in the image of the heavenly beings, among whom God includes himself by the use of the plural pronouns, in Gen. 1:26: "Let us make man in our image, after our likeness." This device carefully guards God's uniqueness by hiding him among the members of his heavenly court and so prevents man and woman from claiming to be exactly like God and thus divine.

48. Contrary to Paul's traditional Jewish views in I Cor. 11:7.

49. We do not move into the realm of actual historical narrative in the Old Testament until we get to Gen., ch. 12. The first eleven chapters are designed as a picture of universal mankind in general. Even from Gen., ch. 12, on, the accounting is always confessional, designed to tell what God has done in the life of his people Israel.

50. We must not push the figure of speech into literalism and conclude that husbands must forgive their wives, but wives have no reason to forgive their husbands. Such is not at all the intent of the passage.

51. Carl Rogers, *On Becoming a Person* (Houghton Mifflin Company, 1961), pp. 122, 119.

52. Rogers, *Becoming Partners,* p. 200.

53. Ellen Goodman. Anderson-Moberg Syndicates, Inc., 1974.

54. Alice Rossi, in Thompson (ed.), *op. cit.*

55. See the Swedish report to the United Nations on "The Status of Women in Sweden," 1968. See also Thompson (ed.), *op. cit.,* pp. 158 ff.

56. Dorothy Dix column, as published in the Lancaster *Intelligencer-Journal.*

57. George Williams, "Creatures of a Creator, Members of a Body, Subjects of a Kingdom," in Theodore A. Gill (ed.), *To God Be the Glory: Sermons in Honor of George Arthur Buttrick* (Abingdon Press, 1973), p. 107.

58. Alice Rossi, quoted in *The National Observer,* March 29, 1965, p. 20.

59. See Karl Menninger's book, *Whatever Became of Sin?* (Hawthorn Books, Inc., 1973), which is actually an agonized moral and profoundly personal protest against our loss of a sense of responsibility to God.

60. David R. Mace, *Whom God Hath Joined* (The Westminster Press, 1953), p. 89.

61. See page 45 f.

62. Rogers, *Becoming Partners,* pp. 213–214.

63. Nena and George O'Neill, *Open Marriage: A New Life Style for Couples* (M. Evans & Co., 1972).

64. *Ibid.,* pp. 84–86.

65. *Ibid.,* p. 257.

66. *Ibid.,* p. 258.

67. George R. Bach and Peter Wyden, *The Intimate Enemy: How to Fight Fair in Love and Marriage* (William Morrow & Company, Inc., 1969), pp. 286–287.

68. Cf. Howard J., Jr., and Charlotte H. Clinebell, *The Intimate Marriage* (Harper & Row, Publishers, Inc., 1970), pp. 68 ff.

69. Edward Carpenter, quoted in Mace, *Whom God Hath Joined,* pp. 26–27.

70. Dr. Jessie Bernard, *Foundations for Christian Family Policy,* as cited by Elizabeth S. and William H. Genné in *Christians and the Crisis in Sex Morality* (Association Press, 1962), pp. 56–58.

71. Temple Gairdner, quoted in Mace, *Whom God Hath Joined,* p. 52.

72. Actually the Biblical definition of a saint, based on the meaning of the verb "to be holy," is one who is set apart by God for a special purpose. In this sense, we all are saints, as Paul for example acknowledges of the unruly and sinful Corinthians (I Cor. 1:2; II Cor. 1:1).

73. As reported by Georgia Dullea for the *New York Times* News Service, July 1, 1975.

74. For brief but good presentations, see Roland H. Bainton, *What Christianity Says About Sex, Love and Marriage* (Association Press, 1957), or David R. Mace, *The Christian Response to the Sexual Revolution* (Abingdon Press, 1970).

75. Bainton, op. cit., pp. 42–43.

76. Ibid., pp. 93 ff.

77. See Mark 2:13–17, 18–22, 23–28 and pars.; 6:30–44 and pars.; 7:1–23, 24–30 and par.; 8:1–10 and par.; 9:49–50; 14:3–9 and par., 17–25 and pars.; Matt. 6:25–34; 22:1–14; Luke 12:35–46 and par.; 14:7–14; 17:7–10; 17:22–37.

78. Karl Barth, Church Dogmatics, III, 4, pp. 133 f.

79. Harvey Cox, The Secular City (The Macmillan Company, 1965), pp. 214–215.

80. John A. T. Robinson, Christian Morals Today (The Westminster Press, 1964), p. 42.

81. I am indebted for these insights concerning the sexual education of children to Helmut Thielicke, The Ethics of Sex (Harper & Row, Publishers, Inc., 1964), pp. 69 ff.

82. Mace, Whom God Hath Joined, p. 39.

83. Bach and Wyden, op. cit., p. 53.

84. Wallace Denton, Family Problems and What to Do About Them (The Westminster Press, 1971), p. 55.

85. Ibid., pp. 66 ff.

86. Gael Green, "Speaking Out: A Vote Against Motherhood," The Saturday Evening Post, Jan. 26, 1963, p. 12.

87. See Bainton, op. cit., pp. 25 ff.

88. Noshpitz, loc. cit.

89. Ibid.

90. Menninger, op. cit.

91. Roy W. Fairchild, Christians in Families (Covenant Life Curriculum, John Knox Press, 1964), pp. 29–30.

92. Phyllis McGinley, Sixpence in Her Shoe (Dell Publishing Co., 1965), p. 229.

93. Noshpitz, loc. cit.

94. Clark Ellzey, "How Far Is a Parent Responsible?" Stephens College Bulletin, Vol. 45, No. 4 (May 1966), p. 32.

Suggestions for Further Reading

Bach, George R., and Wyden, Peter. *The Intimate Enemy: How to Fight Fair in Love and Marriage.* William Morrow & Company, Inc., 1969.

Bowman, Henry A. *Marriage for Moderns.* McGraw-Hill Book Co., Inc., 7th ed., 1974.

Capon, Robert F. *Bed and Board: Plain Talk About Marriage.* Simon & Schuster, Inc., 1965.

Clinebell, Howard J., Jr., and Charlotte H. *The Intimate Marriage.* Harper & Row, Publishers, Inc., 1970.

Denton, Wallace. *Family Problems and What to Do About Them.* The Westminster Press, 1971.

Fairchild, Roy W. *Christians in Families.* Covenant Life Curriculum, John Knox Press, 1964.

Mace, David R. *Whom God Hath Joined.* The Westminster Press, 1953; rev. ed., 1973.

——— and Vera. *We Can Have Better Marriages If We Really Want Them.* Abingdon Press, 1974.

Rogers, Carl R. *Becoming Partners: Marriage and Its Alternatives.* Dell Publishing Co., Inc., 1972.

Shedd, Charlie W. *Letters to Karen: On Keeping Love in Marriage.* Abingdon Press, 1965.

Index of
Biblical References